THE CHALLENGE OF THE SOUL

For Elizabeth & Jerry —

THE
CHALLENGE
—— OF THE ——
SOUL

A Guide for the Spiritual Warrior

RABBI NILES ELLIOT GOLDSTEIN

TRUMPETER
Boston & London
2009

TRUMPETER BOOKS
An imprint of
Shambhala Publications, Inc.
Horticultural Hall
300 Massachusetts Avenue
Boston, Massachusetts 02115
www.shambhala.com

9 8 7 6 5 4 3

Printed in the United States of America

⊗ This edition is printed on acid-free paper that meets the
American National Standards Institute z39.48 Standard.
♻ This book was printed on 100% postconsumer recycled paper.
For more information please visit www.shambhala.com.

Distributed in the United States by Random House, Inc.,
and in Canada by Random House of Canada Ltd

Library of Congress Cataloging-in-Publication Data
Goldstein, Niles Elliot, 1966–
The challenge of the soul: a guide for the spiritual warrior/
Niles Elliot Goldstein.
p. cm.
ISBN 978-1-59030-660-4 (pbk.: alk. paper)
1. Spiritual life—Judaism. 2. Jewish way of life. 3. Conduct of life.
4. Self-actualization (Psychology)—Religious aspects—Judaism.
5. Goldstein, Niles Elliot, 1966–
I. Title.
BM723.G658 2009
296.7'2—dc22
2009009852

This book is dedicated to my family—
Mom, Dad, Caryn, and Daniel

Just as the river where I step
is never the same
yet it is the same river,
so I am
and yet I am never the same.

—HERACLITUS

CONTENTS

THE CHALLENGE OF THE SOUL

INTRODUCTION

ALTHOUGH I HATE TO ADMIT IT, I have become more and more convinced that Thomas Hobbes had it right: human life *is* nasty, brutish, and short.

But so what?

In the end, all we truly have control over are our own souls, and often those souls must fight with themselves in arenas of our own making.

The real issue—and it is a spiritual issue—is how we face up to that hard truth, to the lifelong and, at times, fierce battle between who we are and who we want to be. That struggle can be intense (and, for some of us, stultifying).

As someone who has been both a rabbi and a martial artist for the past fifteen years, I have always been amazed at the striking similarities I've discovered as I continue to pursue these different and seemingly oppositional paths. Whatever weaknesses I possess, or mistakes I make, invariably carry over from one field to the next; whatever teachings, principles, or techniques I learn that advance and expand my skills in one area are inevitably mirrored by advances and growth in the other.

When I earned my black belt in karate just after rabbinic ordination, I had learned not only a particular set of combat skills, but a wide array of tools that would help me in my vocation as a religious teacher and counselor—commitment, patience, humility, the power of repetition and practice, empathy, the ability to channel my strength in positive ways, self-sacrifice. I had also learned to confront—and grow from—some of the darker aspects of my own restless soul—the fears, insecurities, wounds, anger, and occasionally violent impulses that resided in those hidden places within me.

Fighting taught me how to teach.

Like other animals in the natural world, all human beings have a "fight or flight" response embedded deep inside of us. It is our personalities and histories that largely determine toward which of these two poles we are more predisposed, whether when battered and backed into a corner we boldly stand toe-to-toe against our opponents (be they external or internal ones) or decide instead to take a dive.

If, as Carl Jung argued, every human being has a "shadow" within us to confront and contend with, then, in a very real sense, we are *all* engaged in a psychic battle on a daily basis, especially in this troubled and troubling era—and the prize isn't a title or a belt, but a healthy, well-balanced soul. That is a fundamental goal of religion and religious practice, and that has been my own goal and struggle. I have come to the personal conclusion over the years that no theology or spiritual system that discusses God, without equal reference to the development and improvement of the individual spirit, is one that warrants our time, energy, or serious attention.

In Christianity, the image and symbolism of the cross is of paramount importance—it is meant, in part, to teach us about the challenges of being human, but also about the reality of redemption. In classical Islam, the concept of jihad relates, in many understandings, to the *internal* struggle that each of us must go through in order to grow in strength of character and in our relationship to God and others. And in Buddhism, the Four Noble Truths posit that life entails suffering—but that there is a path that allows the resolute (and enlightened) to escape its sting.

Sun Tzu's ancient Chinese manual, *The Art of War,* is read today not just by future officers in military academies but by people the world over as a valuable code of behavior and guide to success, an aid in the way they conduct their lives, their interpersonal relationships, and their work. But the sayings and practices of history's great *spiritual* warriors can do the same thing for modern-day men and women seeking to overcome their fears, empower their souls, and push past their obstacles.

This book's objective is to provide a step-by-step program for contemporary searchers to become spiritual warriors *ourselves.* By interweaving the teachings of sages, mystics, and biblical figures with some of my own insights and personal experiences as a rabbi, seeker, and martial artist, *The Challenge of the Soul* offers a path toward self-empowerment and, ultimately, self-transcendence, a guide toward the inner redemption that so many of us in this disturbing time so desperately crave.

These are the principles, practices, and concepts I have found to be necessary to achieve that goal, which we will explore in the pages ahead:

- Openness
- Introspection
- Discipline
- Courage
- Creativity
- Stamina
- Restraint
- Perseverance

What are the qualities of a spiritual warrior? An understanding of, and mastery over, one's own soul; insight and perspective; a sense of mission.

How do I define the word *soul,* that entity so vital to our path and program? What is its nature and relationship to God? Before I answer that question and starting point, it is worth noting that Aristotle thought that there were actually three different and distinct types of souls that inhere in the world: the nutritive soul (which even plants can possess), the sensitive soul (which is a part of nonhuman animals), and the rational soul (which belongs exclusively to human beings). The hierarchy is clear, and it is also cumulative—while a plant will never get beyond merely trying to nourish and sustain itself, only humanity is capable of self-preservation, sensitivity to and awareness of the world around us, and exercising our minds through the utilization of reason.

As a rabbi, this explanation is not enough for me. It leaves no room for God, or for that relationship with the divine that we often refer to as "spirituality." So I must turn to the Jewish tradition to find both my pedagogic answer and my personal anchor. It is in Jewish mysticism—and in the Kabbalah, specifically—that the soul is explained in a way that rings the most true to me, intellectually and through my own experiences.

The answer can be discovered in the mystical acronym *NaRaN: nefesh, ruach,* and *neshamah,* the three different and interconnected levels of our single soul. Like Aristotle, the Kabbalists believed that the "soul" had a hierarchy of levels. The nefesh, the lowest rung, might be thought of as our life force, our drive to survive and to act (at times, out of more primal impulses and desires). Nefesh is related to how we express ourselves. Ruach, the next and higher level, could be conceived of as our spirit, the conscious reality inside us that yearns to be more than it is, but that also contains within it a spark of divinity. Ruach relates to self-empowerment and self-actualization. The third, highest level of the soul is neshamah, the last link in our invisible chain of being and the one that brings us closest to God. Neshamah is who we are at our most holy. It is not about self-expression or self-realization—it is about the transcendence of the self.

The Gaon of Vilna (1720–1797), one of the most influential rabbinic authorities of all time, was influenced himself by many of the core ideas of the Kabbalah—and that included ideas about the nature of the human soul. The Gaon believed firmly in the tripartite structure of NaRaN, but he believed that it was only at the middle level of the soul—ruach—that human beings lived out their spiritual lives on a daily basis. With nefesh (in all its primitivity) beneath us, and neshamah (in all its transcendent glory) above us, the Gaon claimed that our ruach is in a perpetual tug-of-war with its counterparts, each of which struggles to draw us nearer to it. Which will win? Our drives and feelings at their most base and animalistic, or our higher nature? Pulled in opposite directions, our composite soul, through the use of free will, must choose the overall trajectory of our spiritual development. Often it must fight tooth and nail with itself.

That battle for a balanced, integrated soul is our life's mission. When we have accomplished that integration—when we have expunged or sublimated aspects of nefesh in ways that do not allow them to hold us back from inner growth and, at the same time, tapped into those metaphysical elements of neshamah that hover over us, dormant but waiting—then our soul becomes a healthy, indivisible totality, a conduit for the spiritual light of the Shechinah, the divine presence, to emanate and flow throughout our being. At this point of integration, even the most mundane of our actions become expressions of divinity.

Not everyone is up to this challenge, however. A spiritual warrior understands and accepts this difficult task and grasps its gravity. What more noble purpose could a human being have than to bring the light of God's presence into our darkened world? Yet that can only happen *after* we have worked on ourselves, and that is the reason I have written this book—to help us with our inner work. There is constant crossover among the various levels of the soul, and the chapters that follow will illustrate that phenomenon very clearly. As we examine the lives, ideas, and struggles of others, we will bob and weave between the different rungs of NaRaN, and we will see (despite their interconnection) just how porous and murky the links of the soul, and the spiritual path, can be.

The ring is a symbol of battle. It is also a symbol of union. The dance between combat and communion is a universal one, and the footwork that is frequently required to harmonize these two very different experiences is extremely (some of us would say excruciatingly) difficult to master. Each of us must struggle against, and with, our many and varied opponents—the foes within ourselves as well as those in the office, at home, and that we encounter during the course of our day. The identification of, and engagement with, our real adversaries is the most basic challenge of the human condition.

But we are all in this contest together. Your battle is my battle.

And if, in openness and humility, we can listen to and learn from the words and deeds of those who have danced before us, then at least we'll have a fighting chance.

1

THE POWER OF VULNERABILITY

I SAT ALONE on a bench in the locker room of the dojo in nothing but my boxers. A stiff white robe was draped across my right thigh and a tightly coiled, oversize white belt rested on the concrete floor, as if waiting to be freed from its constricted form.

I started to sweat. What was I about to step into?

In the adjacent room, I could already hear the others warming up—the sound of bags and boards being kicked and punched, of people leaping and landing onto varnished wood, of rubber mats being dragged around, and the occasional violent shout. There was a lot of silence, too, but the experience in its totality was genuinely frightening.

And I was about to step onto that same floor.

TABULA RASA

When I began shopping around Los Angeles for the right dojo and martial arts system and witnessed for the first time the more experienced practitioners (mainly the brown and black belts) in action, I thought they looked liked Jedi masters from one of the *Star Wars* movies. The simple yet exotic robes, the determination in their piercing eyes, the atmosphere of solemnity and reverence that permeated the air of many of the karate schools—the whole gestalt of the thing—came across as otherworldly.

As these men and women performed their kata, or training forms, I was amazed not just at the dexterity and beauty I saw, but at the sheer power that the various moves and motions, contortions and expansions could produce. These were average-looking humans transforming their bodies into superhuman weapons. Yet I sensed no anger or hostility. What I felt instead was a sort of peacefulness, a paradoxical serenity.

I was a second-year rabbinical student, and the scene made me imagine what it might have been like for a disciple to bear witness to some ancient spiritual master "in action," whether that meant engaged in prayer, meditation, or teaching. Stories I'd read about the Jewish sages and mystics now raced through my mind.

I put on my pristine, never-before-used white gi, or uniform, but I couldn't figure out how to tie on the damn belt, a long, thick band of white cloth that had to be wrapped around my waist several times in a very specific way. Nor could I create the uniform's traditional knot, no matter how hard I struggled with it. I was clueless. With practice about to start and with no other choice, I rushed barefoot onto the floor of the dojo, holding the belt feebly in my clammy hand, and approached an instructor for help.

Rather than smirking at me (which I half expected), the instructor gently took my belt and, without uttering a single word, wrapped it effortlessly around my body until it—and the knot—were affixed to my gi precisely as they were supposed to be. Then everyone in the room knelt on the floor for a few moments of silent meditation, bowed toward the head instructor (who bowed back), and began our class.

What I recall most vividly about the session, from getting

8

help with my uniform to making it through my first practice, was the patience shown to me—as well as the desire on the part of my instructors to *teach,* to impart this warrior wisdom and practice to others. Very little of this pedagogic desire, or the training itself, involved any words—just an unspoken understanding and empathy from my teachers about where I was in my training and what I could handle at that juncture in my journey.

I also sensed restraint. There was tremendous power in that room, and I felt it. It was like those bizarre but potent seconds of electrified air you sometimes feel before lightning strikes. I knew there was a world that was being carefully withheld from me, a world of possibility that I'd be exposed to when I was ready.

Although it happened close to two decades ago, "Day One in the Dojo" was a completely virgin experience for me that I will never forget, crammed with raw, primal emotions and sensations (fear, humility, innocence, vulnerability, openness, awe, and an almost boundless feeling of dependence and trust) that I most likely will not—and cannot—encounter again as long as I live.

Not in the same way. Not with such potency.

For the first weeks and months of my karate training, I practiced a rigid dedication, even "religious" devotion, to doing little more than simply learning the fundamentals of this new system. My black belt instructors taught me how to breathe, how to stand, how to develop the proper mindset and attitude when confronted by an opponent. Nothing fancy or acrobatic. Just nuts and bolts.

All of it seemed to complement my seminary studies. The tales I'd read about sages and disciples began to feel more relevant and immediate. Aside from being a great outlet for the pressures of graduate school, karate began to teach me principles and practices that would one day come into play in my work as a rabbi. And it forced me to confront the harsh reality of just how long it takes and how hard it is to strive to master any serious endeavor, particularly those—such as spiritual life and the martial arts—that necessitate making arduous, and at times painful, journeys within ourselves and within our struggling, imperfect, all-too-human souls.

A couple of years later, I found myself yet again holding a strange white robe in one hand and a matching white belt in the other. But this garment wasn't a gi—it was a *kittel,* the traditional (and thankfully lighter) white robe that male Jews wear over their clothing throughout the Days of Awe period, the holiest time of the Jewish year, between Rosh Hashanah and Yom Kippur. It was easier to put on than a gi, but even after four years of rabbinical school, I was still careful to button up and tie the belt of this ceremonial garment in its proper historical sequence and fashion.

After all, I had a congregation to stand in front of.

Like a gi, the kittel is intended to convey innocence, purity, vulnerability, and trust. It is meant to express in an outward and visible way our inner humility, our willingness to stand naked and exposed before God on these days of judgment. According to ancient religious tradition, Jewish men are both married *and* buried in them. The kittel is a symbol of the spiritual journey itself, a celebration of the new year and the gift of life, but also a death shroud, an acknowledgment of our mortality.

That's what I was going to teach the Jews of Indiana, Pennsylvania.

I'd just moved to New York City to continue my graduate studies at one of my seminary's other campuses, driven there by my love for a Princeton woman. We'd dated long-distance during the year I lived in Los Angeles, but the relationship ended pretty soon after I'd landed at La Guardia, when she dumped me. It was ultimately just as well. As the Hasidic rabbi Menachem Mendel of Kotzk, also known as the Kotzker Rebbe (1787–1859), wrote nearly two centuries before, "There is nothing so whole as a heart that has been broken."

My heart had indeed gradually mended from its wound, and the scar tissue felt tender but strong, braced and ready for new adventures (and, inevitably, more potential breakups). As a consequence of the experience as a whole, I'd gained some valuable wisdom about relationships and some key insights into my own personality. After my initial period of brokenness, I'd become more open, more whole, more fully "human"—and more keenly aware of how scary it can be, and the genuine risks that are involved, when we allow someone else to enter deeply into our soul.

I'd also found a wonderful new dojo, affiliated with my Shotokan karate style. My learning and lessons continued without interruption in that arena, too.

By day, I put on my yarmulke and studied the Bible, medieval commentaries, the Talmud, Jewish law, Midrash, and pastoral counseling. At night, I put on my well-worn gi (now that I knew how to), stepped barefoot onto the dojo floor, and studied the martial arts. On most weekends, I took a flight to Pittsburgh, rented a car, then drove up to Indiana, Pennsylvania, where I served as that Jewish community's student rabbi. Head and heart, body and soul—everything I did back then felt integrated and interwoven. Each activity played a vital role in the journey I was on.

I learned a great deal about being a congregational rabbi in that out-of-the-way town, home to a university and of the legendary actor, Jimmy Stewart (I seem to recall a statue of him that stood somewhere near city hall). I was busily immersed in my clerical field training, learning the fundamentals of the Jewish spiritual system: leading Shabbat services, directing and teaching in the religious school, trying to help people with their personal problems. As was the case with my initial encounter with karate, over the course of time—and with patience and practice—all that I did as a young rabbinical student became easier and more comfortable for me. Intimidation and insecurity eventually gave way to confidence as I allowed myself to open up to the possibilities of my new role in a community.

One of my major responsibilities as that community's student rabbi was to lead services and preach sermons during the

Days of Awe, the most sacred period of the Jewish year. It is a high-pressure time for Jewish clergy, when Jews across the world come out of the woodwork, when those who ordinarily wouldn't be caught dead in a synagogue or at services decide to show up to usher in the New Year and to ask forgiveness for their transgressions from the year that's just past. It's a time when Jews fill pews, and it's an opportunity for rabbis to teach, inspire, and challenge them.

That is what I wanted to do by wearing a kittel before my student congregation all those years ago. It was my first time to do so, and I've worn one every year since. Yet because the kittel is strongly associated with Orthodox Judaism, it was virtually unheard of for a future Reform rabbi (such as I was) to don such an "antiquated" garment. Even today, in most nontraditional Jewish contexts, witnessing a service leader wearing a kittel would be like catching a glimpse of bigfoot—a rare sight, for sure.

I was viewed immediately as a provocateur, all the more so because I hadn't yet been formally ordained. Despite some discomfort at the reaction I could see in the eyes of my congregants, I'd already achieved my objective, even before I'd uttered the opening prayer. I *did* want to make a point, an unmistakable, in-your-face kind of point: For me, all of this religion "stuff" was profoundly serious, and very much a matter of life and death. I wasn't merely going to go through the liturgical motions during these Days of Awe; I was going to make a spiritual pilgrimage into the deepest and darkest parts of my very soul, and I was challenging the congregation to join me on the journey.

I didn't have to say a single word to convey that message.

Though they end with Yom Kippur, the Day of Atonement, the Days of Awe begin with Rosh Hashanah, the Jewish New Year. Rosh Hashanah is a time for joy and gratitude, but it is also a time—as the words of the liturgy imply—for openness and receptivity. At several points in the prayer book, we read the following line: *Hayom harat olam* ("This is the day of the world's birth"). And the rabbis who composed that line meant it. God didn't just create the world as a one-time event and then disappear—God actively renews the work of creation every year, every day, every instant. Rosh Hashanah may be the fixed ceremonial period when we reaffirm this truth through rituals, customs, and prayers, but the constancy at the core is what really matters.

Life isn't a given—it is a gift. Each moment that we breathe presents us with the opportunity for renewal and transformation.

In all that we do, we must begin at the beginning. And the Days of Awe, particularly Rosh Hashanah, teach us that it is *always* the beginning.

And so we venture ever forward into the unknown and unknowable future, aware that anything can happen to anyone at any time.

Does that mean we have to live in fear and dread? Not at all. It means, if we are up to the challenge, that we need to approach life as warriors—prepared, attuned, open to every moment, ready and receptive to whatever might come our way.

EMBRACING OUR INNOCENCE

The German lyric poet Rainer Maria Rilke writes that "beauty is nothing but the beginning of terror." I know from firsthand experience that witnessing a master martial artist perform an intricate kata with majestic precision, or being exposed to a profound mystical text from the Kabbalah, can be absolutely awe inspiring. It might even induce a feeling of fear and trembling. That's why it is so vital to be open, to trust our teachers—and ourselves. Intimidation is an impediment to growth. It takes courage to step onto the floor of a dojo for the first time, or to look at a page from a seemingly incomprehensible book that other people study with apparent ease on a daily basis.

Our feeling of vulnerability will dissipate with time, but we must go through it. And we must embrace our innocence as if it were *itself* a teacher.

Innocence doesn't come easily. I have long been fascinated by the figure of Rabbi Shimon ben Lakish, an important Jewish sage who, prior to becoming a rabbinic scholar, fought as a gladiator under Roman rule more than fifteen hundred years ago. Although Resh Lakish (as he is commonly known) is cited in the Talmud and other rabbinic literature on many occasions, very little is known of his gladiatorial days. He himself says next to nothing about them directly.

Yet anyone who has ever studied his profound teachings can't help but feel an underlying sensitivity that must have emerged from his brutal experience as a professional fighter, a tenderness and vulnerability of spirit that influenced his sharp intellect and informed his compelling, often stark insights. Resh Lakish, performing half-naked before the masses, faced life and death struggles for years. Once he was freed of his gladiatorial obligations, however, it became clear to him that the combat-warrior path could not nourish his soul. Resh Lakish abandoned the world of the arenas. His fidelity and self-submission was not to any emperor or ancient superpower.

It was to God.

This is not the image that most of us today have of the gladiator. That image has been shaped by Hollywood, by actors such as Kirk Douglas (*Spartacus*) and Russell Crowe (*Gladiator*). These films portray both historical and imagined freedom fighters, men bent on breaking Rome's yoke and motivated by the human desire for political freedom. Resh Lakish, in rejecting the coliseum and embracing the yeshiva, was motivated by the equally human yearning to smash the bonds of finitude, to bring his will into alignment with that of the divine—and to achieve transcendence in the process.

His blood-stained broadswords, tridents, and armor were eventually supplanted by the rites, rituals, and ceremonies of religion and religious life. Resh Lakish may have carried the burden of ugly scars and terrible memories with him on the road to his inner transformation, but he also brought with him invaluable experience and knowledge. He exposed himself to the rigors and challenges of both worlds—and he chose the spiritual one, bringing with him an openness and humility that would lead him to great depth.

According to Resh Lakish, "The proselyte is dearer to God than was the entire household of Israel when it was gathered together at Mount Sinai." What does he mean? It is one thing to be born into a community or a faith. It is something very different—and a much harder, more intimidating step—to *choose* to become one of its members and practitioners. Though Resh Lakish was born a Jew, he surely had a "conversion" experience at some stage during his days in the coliseum, one that propelled him from the fierce but familiar world of combat into the unknown terrain of rabbis and religiosity.

His words seem to suggest that God cares most for those who care most deeply, those who venture forth with passion and abandon—fresh and free of coercion—and align themselves not only with the divine, but with a new community, belief system, and discipline. God favors the student, the person who, in complete innocence, demonstrates sincere devotion to learning from others, to training in a zone of *discomfort* about which he or she knows next to nothing. That in itself is an expression of openness and love.

We can never return to, or relive, our "virgin" moments: going to an overnight camp for the first time, experiencing our first day as a freshman at college, meeting our first love, taking our first step into a martial arts school or a rabbinical seminary. Those are powerful, energy-filled events, and at the time we went through them, they may have even scared us. With the passage of time, though, all we can hold on to are our memories of them.

I know people who have practiced the martial arts for decades, and members of the clergy who have served congregations for half their lives. Some of them have utterly lost the spark that ignited their initial passion for those pursuits. Now I watch them just going through the motions, like zombies. They look bored and tired, and it saddens me. I am on a never-ending quest for innocence, for openness to the unknown, so that the same fate does not befall me.

The challenge of a spiritual warrior is to treat every situation as if it is brand new, to draw excitement from the familiar and exhilaration from the mundane. Each moment presents us with an opportunity to become zealous and energetic "proselytes" all over again, to treat life's many and varied experiences as first-time, conversion-like events. Striving to engender in ourselves a condition of perpetual innocence—of wonder and amazement about even the most ordinary of activities or contexts—is not easy. That's why finding renewal in repetition is a *skill,* both in combat and in spiritual growth, and it is one that must be cultivated, nurtured, and developed through our training.

The fruits of this skill are, ultimately, community and communion—and an openness and receptivity so profound and powerful as to transform our souls.

OPENNESS TO TRANSCENDENCE

When I speak with artists, writers, and composers, they frequently describe their work not as something that they achieve, but rather something that they receive. While it is common for religious mystics to describe experiences of having their souls possessed by the divine spirit, even atheists in the creative fields talk about the role of the muse as the mysterious source that inspires their craft. This shouldn't surprise us. The etymological root of the word inspiration means "the internalization of spirit"—for that to occur, though, we must be open and receptive to it. The borders between creative inspiration and spiritual revelation are much more porous than most of us think.

· The Sabbath highlights this point. Erich Fromm, the important countercultural psychoanalyst, discusses in his book *You Shall Be As Gods* how the Sabbath embodies that same synthesis of the material and the spiritual. The Sabbath—arguably the key observance in biblical religion—is an expression of freedom in its fullest form. Yet it is a freedom anchored firmly in the ideas of giving up and of giving *over.*

The Sabbath, in traditional Judaism and Christianity, is a day when we are supposed to refrain from work. Why? By not working, Fromm observes, we are no longer participants in, nor are we bound by, the process of natural and social change. This "frees" us from the limitations of time—for just one day a week. The Sabbath represents messianic time, providing us, if we choose to accept it, with a taste of eternity.

It is not work or production that is the paramount value for Fromm, but rest. In the context of the Sabbath, it is this state of rest that sets us free, that humanizes us, that allows us to experience life in its purist manifestation. It has no other purpose, nor does it strive for one. As a humanist and a clinician, Fromm must have seen the Sabbath as a very effective vehicle for both character development and self-actualization.

Yet there are other, more metaphysical (and even mystical) ways to view the Sabbath, and Abraham Joshua Heschel, an influential modern rabbi and activist, offers us one in his book *The Sabbath*. For him, unlike Fromm, the Sabbath synthesizes the psycho-spiritual *and* the aesthetic. On that holy day, each of us is given the opportunity to act as an artisan of the soul, to participate in the creation of what Heschel calls "a palace in time." That spiritual architecture, however, is contingent on our working to construct it: without its builders doing their job, the palace cannot come into existence. The paradox of the Sabbath is that our "work" and our freedom are the consequence of merely being. When we take up residence in the palace, and when we allow the palace to dwell inside us, we create a harmony of mind and spirit, of human and divine.

We live fully in the moment, in the eternal now.

Some religious thinkers, such as Søren Kierkegaard, the nineteenth-century existentialist, argue that authentic faith (and the inner rewards that flow from it) requires that we make a leap into a world of uncertainty, that we embrace an attitude of absolute resignation about our capacity to grasp the transcendent mystery of God: "Infinite resignation is the last stage before faith," he writes in *Fear and Trembling*, "for only in infinite resignation do I become conscious of my eternal validity, and only then can one speak of grasping existence by virtue of faith." This act of surrender is active rather than passive, an expression of courage and strength rather than fear and weakness. What it represents is an affirmation of our fundamental, though finite, humanity.

Fromm, a staunch nonmystic, refers to infinite resignation as possessing the "x attitude." He claims that, whether or not there is a God, cultivating this kind of an attitude toward life and the world can be of immense benefit to us as human beings, for it results in "a letting go of one's 'ego,' one's greed, and with it, of one's fears; a giving up the wish to hold onto the 'ego' as if it were an indestructible, separate entity; a making oneself empty in order to be able to fill oneself with the world, to respond to it, to become one with it, to love it. To make oneself empty does not express passivity but *openness.*"

It is only when we empty ourselves and give over, when our dreams and desires become intertwined with those of the divine, that our lives can take on a freer and more fulfilling dimension. Relinquishing our preoccupation with self and accepting the constraints of our "mortal coil" (to cite Shakespeare) are not easy tasks, but what we receive in return is a renewed, deeper, and more meaningful existence.

The paradox of being a spiritual warrior is that the channels for our strength originate in places we don't ordinarily expect them to. Yet it is precisely in these areas—emptiness, openness, and receptivity—that we can discover tremendous reservoirs of power. The Hebrew word *Kabbalah,* for instance, one of the great (and probably best known) of the Jewish mystical movements, translates as "that which is received." To put it another way, genuine mystical experience is something that *comes* to us, not something that we can go out and "get." It is the result of giving over, not of giving up.

This receiving involves a lot of hard work. When we learn (and train) to inculcate these mindsets and attitudes within ourselves, we will gain freedom, power, and the confidence to confront new situations and challenges, however daunting they may seem.

As a well-traveled rabbi who had visited Jews and Jewish communities from Fairbanks, Alaska, to Port Douglas, Australia, I thought I'd seen it all. I'd witnessed religious customs and traditions from all over the world, some of them familiar (such as lighting Sabbath candles at a home in Rio de Janeiro) and some of them new and a bit disconcerting (such as being served the decapitated head of a carp for dinner on a Friday night by a Yemenite family). But officiating at a Bukharan wedding ceremony in Kew Gardens, Queens—of all places—beat out all of them by a pretty good margin. And it taught me that among the customs of at least one Jewish ethnic group, a symbolic expression of openness and vulnerability is one of the very first acts that a new couple must make before they embark on their journey together through life.

Right before my fifth and final year of rabbinical school, I spent the summer traveling through Central Asia, a remote and exotic region of nomads, horsemen, and the ancient Silk Road. It was 1993. All three of the countries that I visited—Kazakhstan, Kyrgyzstan, and Uzbekistan—hadn't even existed until a year earlier, having been republics in the former Soviet Union. My mission was to bring Judaism to Jews—Jews who had been prevented from openly practicing their religion under Soviet rule. I led services, went with mourners to say prayers at the graves of family members, and lectured on Jewish history, among other activities. It was all so fascinating and fulfilling to me. It felt like religion in the raw. There I was, feeding the hungry souls of men and women who had been denied their spiritual sustenance for decades.

I met with Jews of all different ethnic backgrounds. Under Stalin, they'd been sent to Central Asia from places as far away as East Germany, Poland, the Ukraine, and elsewhere, in his efforts to "Sovietize" every citizen by whitewashing their geographical, cultural, and religious distinctions. In Uzbekistan, though, I visited one community of Jews who seemed to have successfully thwarted Stalin's efforts.

The Bukharan Jews (their name derives from the ancient town of Bukhara) trace their ancestry to the Babylonian exile, over 2,500 years ago. While their history is a matter of scholarly dispute, the Bukharans have lived in the region of modern Uzbekistan for many centuries. They are a small community when compared to Ashkenazi Jews, like myself, who have family roots in large swaths of Eastern Europe, but they are very proud of their traditions, many of which are unique to them.

Today, most of the Bukharan Jews I met in Uzbekistan have moved either to Israel or to the United States, and there is a strong, tightly-knit population of them in New York City (particularly in the Kew Gardens neighborhood of Queens).

So when I received a call several years ago from Misha, a Bukharan friend who'd immigrated to Kew Gardens not long after my visit to Samarkand (his birthplace and the religious and cultural center of the Bukharan community the world over), I wasn't that surprised to hear from him. And I was extremely honored when he asked if I would officiate at the wedding ceremony of his oldest daughter in their new apartment.

"But I'm not Bukharan," I said, knowing how unusual it was for an outsider to play such an important role in the insular Bukharan community.

"You are still rabbi," he replied in heavily accented English.

The ceremony was beautiful. Misha had set up the chuppah, or marriage canopy, in the middle of their living room, and the young couple and I were surrounded by family and friends. I went through the standard set of blessings and prayers. About halfway through the ritual, however, something quite unfamiliar started to take place.

Out of the blue, the bridegroom began to unzip his pants. I tried not to notice and continued reading. But then he opened his fly completely, letting the flaps of his dress pants dangle over his thighs and exposing his underwear to the entire room. Nobody seemed to pay attention or care. It was if he were merely clearing his throat.

Okay, I thought to myself, *this guy is a new immigrant, and it is pretty hot in here with all these people around. Maybe he's just nervous and trying to ventilate.*

As I neared the conclusion of the ceremony, the bridegroom zipped his pants back up as if nothing out of the ordinary had occurred. Then it dawned on me. Nothing unusual *had* occurred—at least not in a Bukharan wedding. I'd witnessed a new (but probably very ancient) Jewish religious tradition I'd never seen before, and as I reflected on its symbolism and most likely meaning, the whole thing eventually made sense.

In the very last moments before a spiritual union between this couple could take place, the bridegroom had to show, in a public way, that he had absolutely nothing to hide or to fear, that he was exposed, vulnerable, but ready to face their future.

By allowing himself to be truly open, through an overt (as well as metaphorical) act, this young man was following the way of the warrior, whether he knew it or not.

THE POWER OF OPENNESS

We should never underestimate the elemental power that inheres within our openness, within the dynamic way that "emptying" ourselves (of ego, greed, and fear) allows us to become more receptive to the rewards of the spirit—and the flesh.

A spiritual warrior likely unknown to anyone outside of martial arts circles is Gichin Funakoshi, one of karate's great masters. Born in 1868 in Okinawa, he studied karate from childhood and then organized some of its very first public demonstrations. That in itself was a very bold act on the part of Master Funakoshi, since karate-do (the "way" of karate, the system's more formal title and translation) was a combat art shrouded in secrecy, and almost no records of its early history, which date back more than a thousand years to the Shaolin Temple in Hunan Province, China, existed.

As president of the Okinawa Association for the Spirit of Martial Arts, Master Funakoshi was chosen to demonstrate karate-do at a major athletic exhibition in Tokyo in 1922. This led to the introduction of the ancient martial art to the rest of Japan and, subsequently, to the rest of the world. Other combat styles and systems followed.

Master Funakoshi was a prolific author, but a central theme that he always returns to in his writing is the underlying importance of spirituality and humility. He writes: "True karate-do places weight on spiritual rather than physical matters. True karate-do is this: that in daily life, one's mind and body be trained and developed in a spirit of humility."

If the Japanese word *do* refers to the way, or path, of the spiritual warrior, then what does the word *kara* in karate mean? According to Master Funakoshi, "The first connotation of [the Japanese symbol] kara indicates that karate is a technique that permits one to defend himself with his bare hands and fists and without weapons." But that is only karate at its most basic level. Master Funakoshi continues: "Second, just as it is the clear mirror that reflects without distortion, or the quiet valley that echoes a sound, so must one who would study karate-do purge himself of selfish and evil thoughts, for only with a clear mind and conscience can he understand that which he receives. This is another meaning of the element of kara in karate-do."

Openness, which arises from self-purification, is what leads to receptivity. It is our first step toward letting the lessons of this powerful art sink into us.

The third meaning of kara is the most profound—and the most difficult to fathom. Master Funakoshi writes: "Finally, in a fundamental way, the form of the universe is emptiness (kara), and, thus, emptiness is form itself. There are many kinds of martial arts—judo, kendo, tae kwon do, and others—but at a fundamental level all these arts rest on the same basis as karate-do. Form is emptiness, emptiness is form itself."

Karate is sometimes called the art of the open, or empty, hand. While there are indeed many different hand techniques I've learned in my own years of training (the hammer fist, knuckle punch, and sword hand are just a few of them), I think that the emptiness referred to by Master Funakoshi has more to do with our internal state of soul than it does with anything of a physical nature. Kara, emptiness, is our ultimate key to personal renewal and transformation.

At the deepest level, there *are* no boundaries between emptiness and fullness, metaphysical and physical, soul and body. Yet another paradox for the potential warrior to reflect on during his or her spiritual journey.

VULNERABILITY AND RISK

Many of the ideas in this chapter go back as far as the Bible itself, especially if one is thoughtful and perceptive enough to excavate them from their context in the fascinating but violent world of the ancient Near East. Look at the example of the prophet Ezekiel, a figure not usually thought of as a warrior in any way (as are Samson, Joshua, and David, who were more overtly "martial" in their actions and attitudes). His behavior is extreme, and in most cases inadvisable, but it is illuminating nonetheless. I first discussed Ezekiel in my book *Craving the Divine*. The prophet's life and actions are so relevant to our current topic that I would like to explore him even further here.

Ezekiel, along with most of his fellow Israelites, was dragged into exile by the Babylonians in 598 B.C.E. He lived in relative anonymity with his displaced people along the Chebar River until, several years later, the heavens opened up and Ezekiel received a vision of divinity. It is an unforgettable vision, both powerful and strange: a vivid image of a sapphire throne soaring through the sky, pulled by winged, four-faced creatures; wheels made of flames; clouds, ice, and fire; and a deafening noise.

This vision of what came to be known as the Divine Chariot is so impenetrable and overwhelming that, upon seeing it, Ezekiel collapses on the ground—an expression of humility and submission as much as of perplexity and terror. This is probably not the picture that most of us have in our heads of how a warrior ought to behave. And yet Ezekiel follows the path of a spiritual warrior with understanding and courage.

How could that be? Because what the prophet falls down and submits to is God's unfathomable infinity in contrast to his own imperfect and vulnerable humanity. Ezekiel's behavior is an external reaction to his internal realization that, ultimately, even a visionary prophet is constrained by the limits of the human mind—some things are simply unknowable to us. Ezekiel, unable to penetrate the secrets of the Divine Chariot, jettisons his ego and transforms himself into a *vessel* for the divine message. Like other prophets before him, Ezekiel gives himself over to, and is possessed by, the Transcendent. Now he is prepared to receive and transmit God's holy words.

Ezekiel receives his commission in a compelling way, one that again makes use of the imagery of humility and submission. God commands Ezekiel: "'And you, son of man, hear what I say to you: Be not rebellious, like the rebellious house. Open your mouth and eat what I give you.' And I looked, and behold, a hand was stretched out to me, and behold, it held a written scroll. And he spread it before me, and it had writing on the front and on the back, and there were written on it words of lamentation and mourning and woe. And he said to me, 'Son of man, eat this scroll.' So I opened my mouth and he gave me the scroll to eat, and he said to me, 'Son of man, let your body eat and fill your stomach with this scroll that I give you, and go, speak to the house of Israel!' Then I ate it, and it was in my mouth as sweet as honey" (Ezekiel 2:8–10; 3:1–3).

Although Ezekiel is "force-fed" the words he is to convey to his rebellious people—a result of his surrender to God's will— the prophet's open mouth is a metaphor for his openness and trust. This experience is a cause for delight, not dread.

The honey-sweet scroll he is given becomes nourishment for his soul.

One lesson of this bizarre scene seems to be that spiritual elevation and power come, paradoxically, through *surrender.* After his sacrifice of self, Ezekiel says: "Spirit lifted me up, and I heard behind me a great noise, as the glory of God arose from its place. . . . But spirit lifted me up and took me away, and I went lifted up in the air and greatly moved in spirit, the hand of God being strong upon me" (Ezekiel 3:12, 14).

Words matter. Ezekiel's experience of spiritual communion is an extreme one, in that his physical body becomes enmeshed with the words committed to him—they are literally a part of his flesh and blood. The divine spirit that now inhabits Ezekiel's soul transports him from location to location throughout the story that follows.

Ezekiel makes the very active decision to "empty" himself, and it is because of that bold choice that the divine spirit can enter and animate him. Allowing himself to become an instrument for God leads to a mixed outcome. The prophet must deal with frustration and pain as he tries to transmit God's words of rebuke to a community that will not hear him. Yet Ezekiel also experiences the bliss of self-transcendence as the burden of independence gives way to integration with the divine.

Choosing self-surrender over self-control has been the way of prophets, mystics, and spiritual warriors since time immemorial, and it is not an easy path to follow. But it is a path and a model that has much to teach us as we each struggle to grow and to discover our own direction and purpose. As Master Funakoshi would write many centuries after the Bible, when we strive mightily for this level of depth, there are no boundaries between emptiness and fullness, metaphysical and physical, soul and body.

It is vulnerability that allows us to become more open human beings, that helps us to create the space though which new forces can find their way inside us in ways that enrich and empower our minds, bodies, and souls. And so I want to close this chapter with a few additional thoughts on the spirit and the body—as well as on the great energy and strength we can develop when we are able to harmonize them into a totality.

The image of the Divine Chariot appears once more in the Bible, in the book of Daniel, a later biblical prophet, and it is strikingly similar to the image from Ezekiel. Yet a fascinating element that is unique to Daniel's vision of the chariot (also referred to as the Throne of Glory) is the *Nahar Dinur,* the River of Fire. We learn in the prophet's own colorful description of an "ancient of days . . . whose garment was white as snow, and the hair of whose head was like pure wool; his throne was fiery flames, its wheels burning fire. A river of fire issued and came forth before him" (Daniel 7:9–10).

Many Jewish mystics interpreted this holy fire as the sweat of the creatures that had to hold up and carry the Throne of Glory. In their view, when our own spiritual practices rise to a "fever pitch"—a consequence of emotional zeal and religious commitment—our sweaty bodies are bathed in that same fiery energy.

I have witnessed and experienced that animal-like sweat, both in the synagogue and in the dojo. Whether the result of intense prayer or training, it is dramatic and powerful. And it correlates directly to the devotion of the practitioner.

In the Bible, God is sometimes referred to as *Aish Ochlah,* a "Consuming Fire." To be swallowed by God is to reunite the human soul with its transcendent source. Yet that can only occur when we vacate ourselves of ego, of the narrowness of self-concern. The Kotzker Rebbe, whom we quoted earlier, asks the question: "Where is it that God can be found?" His answer: "Wherever we create the space for God to enter."

We become "chariots" or "thrones" for God only when we make room for the divine to dwell within us. That is the challenge of a spiritual warrior.

To work toward that goal, we must cultivate the courage to surrender, to expose ourselves—through trust—to the unknown. We've all heard the cliché about the calm before the storm, and I think that there is much truth to it. I have always associated those individuals who have intimidated me most with a sense of serenity. I've faced black belts in the dojo whose tranquil eyes both hid, and helped to generate, remarkable expressions of whirlwind skill and terrific strength. And I have learned sacred texts and techniques from religious teachers whose peaceful outer demeanors masked a dizzying inner wisdom and spiritual power that was decidedly awe inspiring.

Yet my most dreaded opponent has usually been myself.

The spiritual warrior must be willing to take risks, especially the risk of vulnerability. It is then, when we have opened ourselves up, that we will start to feel the sudden irruption of our own hidden capacity for power. It is through that fresh void that—like the rush of water through a hole in a dam—confidence will triumph over fear, and hope will vanquish despair.

2

SHADOWBOXING

THE ROOM WAS STARK and crowded. In front of me were two men in uniform, with badges and handguns, and another person behind a desk quietly doing paperwork. Next to me was an assortment of strangers who appeared to have come from nearly every walk of life, and none of them looked as if they wanted to be there. Some seemed nervous and jittery. I sat patiently, but with increasing anxiety, on a hard wooden bench. We had all been instructed earlier that nobody could leave the room under any circumstances until their name was called, and that there were toilets in the back. I felt powerless.

If I hadn't been arrested and jailed those many years before, jury duty probably wouldn't have triggered such uncomfortable feelings. While others read the *New York Post* or toyed with their cell phones, I was transported back to the Tombs, to the cells packed with prisoners that I knew were on the basement floors beneath my feet.

THE DEMONS WITHIN

About a week before I graduated from college—some two decades ago, though it seems like yesterday—I went with a rugby teammate of mine to spend a weekend of partying and celebrating our rite of passage in Manhattan. On that Saturday night, we decided to check out a trendy club in Midtown. A woman I'd been interested in since the instant I'd walked through the front entrance was now buying me shots of scotch. I couldn't have felt more contented. As the two of us stood together at the bar, and as I watched my friend schmooze up a beautiful young woman himself just a few feet away, all seemed right with my world. I was free and without responsibilities, and nothing felt out of reach. It was as if this moment, and the fleshpots of youth, would last forever.

The liquor started to kick in, and eventually I had to take a bathroom break. I excused myself from the woman. After taking several steps away from the bar, though, and vanishing into the crowd, I stopped and surveyed the nightclub. I observed all the young and beautiful people: they were drinking, flirting, and dancing, as if they, too, believed that this moment was never going to end. Suddenly, something unexpected rose up inside of me. It was an overwhelming sense of doom. Like an obsessive thought, a single fact banged against my skull over and over: *everybody here is going to die.*

Why didn't anyone else seem to notice? Why didn't anyone else care?

I detached completely from the reality of the room—from the excitement, the celebration, the atmosphere of self-satisfaction. All I could focus on was my mortality, the irrevocable fact of my finitude. As fun as this party was, I knew inside that it would come to an end—that *we* would end. I did not want to go gently into that good night. I could see through this scene. I could make out the skeletons underneath the Prada.

People were turning into ghosts before my eyes.

My insides quivered with rage and dread; I was frozen in

place until it felt as if I'd explode. Eventually, I pulled myself away from the spectacle and reached the bathroom. There, with nothing but my dark ruminations and for no specific reason, I lashed out, ripping a marble urinal out of the wall and shattering it on the floor. Within minutes, I was grabbed by a group of burly bouncers and hauled upstairs. The police arrived quickly. I was cuffed, placed into a squad car, and driven to a nearby precinct house.

My minor outburst led to a charge of criminal mischief. After my fingerprints had been taken, I was put back in the squad car and driven from the precinct house to the barbed-wire confines of central booking, where I joined other creatures of the night for further processing: photographs, paperwork, cavity searches. I sat for hours, handcuffed and scared. In my mind, I created various scenarios and rehearsed what I'd do to defend myself if someone were to attack me. Lots of kicks, elbows, and knee strikes.

After several more hours of sitting and waiting, my name was finally called, along with about ten others. We were shackled together and led, single file, into a waiting paddy wagon. The first prisoners inside the vehicle got to sit on a bench, but the rest of us had to stand. While the wagon sped through the city, those of us who were standing bounced off the walls like meat carcasses. When we came to a halt, I peered through an air vent and saw my next stop: the Manhattan Criminal Court Building.

For the next twenty-six hours, I was a denizen of New York's infamous Tombs, a labyrinth of old, disgusting holding cells beneath the courtrooms where we'd each plead our individual cases. It is the limbo of the city's penal system. In the Tombs, you wait to see a legal aid lawyer and a judge, and then you're either released onto the streets or sent on to Rikers Island to await trial.

By the end, the experience didn't feel like punishment for my criminal misbehavior, and any of my rage had long since disappeared. I hadn't entered a netherworld—it had entered me. The Tombs were a metaphor and a mirror, an external manifestation of the internal state of my frightened, tortured, and shackled soul. *That* was my real prison.

As a first-time offender, I was released from jail and my charges were ultimately dismissed. Yet I continue, to this very day, to fight the forces that sent me there.

I have learned over time that my true enemies that night, now twenty years behind me, were my own fury and fear. I am mature enough to recognize that my purposeless outburst of violence, rooted in an inability to accept my finitude, was a kind of revelation, perhaps even a gift. I'd been given a glimpse of the darkness within me, as well as its potential consequences. And I have come to realize that unless we can learn to accept, and embrace, our fundamental humanity—with all of its limitations, imperfections, and transitory nature—we will doom ourselves to dwell in prisons of our own making.

While an essential first step in the journey, it is not enough for the aspiring spiritual warrior to nurture and develop the trust that is necessary to open up to new teachers, traditions, and experiences. After openness must come true introspection, making a pilgrimage inside ourselves and taking a long, honest look at what we find there. It won't always be pretty, but we have to know who we are and what raw materials we have to work with if we are ever to become *better* than we are. We must learn to face—and engage—the shadow side, our own inner demons. While these demons are many, I have found anger and fear to be among the most important, elemental, and formidable.

ANGER

Anger is a common impulse that most of us are justifiably wary of, one that we do not ordinarily see as containing much that could help in the maturation of our souls or the betterment of the world. Yet the great psychoanalyst Carl Jung was absolutely convinced that human beings must recognize and embrace the "shadow" dimension inside of us if we are to make progress in the area of our own self-understanding. The darker impulses (such as lust, jealousy, and others) relate to emotion and instinct; they are not things that we do, but things that *happen* to us.

These kinds of impulses are, on one level, manifestations of weaknesses or deficiencies in our personalities, and they take place in the primal region of the unconscious. But, as Jung writes in *The Essential Jung*, the shadow is a very ambiguous part of the human psyche, "on one side regrettable and reprehensible weakness, on the other side healthy instinctivity and the prerequisite for higher consciousness." While at times disconcerting, the shadow is also a repository for potentially constructive, transformational experiences.

Jung believed that too many of the classical religious traditions (Christianity in particular) viewed human nature as dualistic and denigrated the shadow aspect of our souls as the source of all that was evil. He rejected this notion as false and simplistic. From Jung's perspective, there can be no reality without polarity, no light without darkness. What we refer to as our dark side consists not only of base, negative, and harmful inclinations, but also a valuable proportion of positive qualities, such as appropriate responses, realistic assessments, creative drives, and normal instincts.

If we learn to utilize our shadow properly—and this is by no means an easy feat—it can enrich, enliven, and empower us. Trying to suppress it will never work anyway. In *The Essential Jung*, Jung writes that suppression of the shadow is an exercise in futility and foolishness, "as little of a remedy as beheading would be for a headache."

There *is* an appropriate place in our lives for shadow emotions such as anger. More than my harrowing experience in the Tombs, anger itself served as the vehicle that ultimately taught me a critical lesson about my own inner struggles at a key point in my young life and helped me to become a stronger, more mature person.

Anger has also played a vital role in the lives and work of significant figures from the Bible. The Israelite prophets appear for the first time prior to the establishment of a unified monarchy under Saul in approximately 1020 B.C.E. Some of them traversed the land in small groups, prophesying in ecstatic frenzies. One of their primary functions within biblical society was, it seems, to inspire their countrymen to rise up and fight God's holy war against their nemesis, the Philistines. Many prophets lived in communes, not infrequently in the vicinity of a sacred site and often led by a revered master.

In the wake of a bitter civil war in 921 B.C.E. that divided the monarchy into northern and southern kingdoms, another type of prophet came onto the scene. This prophetic model did not follow the ecstatic tradition, nor did this prophet belong to an organized community. In contrast to his predecessors, he was a lone individual who had been called to carry out a specific mission: to deliver a message from God, one that the recipients often did not want to hear. These "classical" prophets (first Amos, then Hosea in northern Israel, followed by Isaiah and Micah in the southern region of Judah) began to emerge in the middle and latter part of the eighth century B.C.E., a period of great prosperity and military strength—as well as widespread social and moral decay.

Even in the face of callousness toward the poor, indifference to the weak, immorality, corruption, disregard for covenantal laws, and the infiltration of pagan practices into the national religion, there is no evidence of protest against the ruling authorities from the political or spiritual figures of the era. It was in this context—and vacuum of moral leadership—that the classical prophets came into being. What the Israelites needed weren't seers or healers, but impassioned, godly men to serve as their society's conscience.

The life of the prophet Jeremiah (645–580 B.C.E.) spanned a particularly critical period in the history of Judah, the southern part of the divided Israelite kingdom. With the exception of a very brief period of independence, Judah had essentially devolved from a regional power into a vassal state and a political pawn under the successive empires of Assyria, Egypt, and Babylonia. The northern kingdom of Israel no longer existed—it had fallen to the Assyrians a century before Jeremiah was even born.

A weak and wounded Judah was all that remained of a once mighty, united Jewish nation. But it, too, was about to make a last stand. Jeremiah would bear witness to its tragic destruction and journey with his people into exile. He would be the monarchy's final prophet.

As fiery advocates of social justice and spiritual rectitude, the classical prophets often spoke in voices filled with fury, and Jeremiah is no exception. He sees Judah's weakness and impending doom as the result of its own sinfulness and internal rot, not as a consequence of anything external, such as geopolitics. Judah has no one to blame but itself for what is about to befall it. When the prophet receives his call and commission, God warns him: "From the north will disaster be loosed upon all who dwell in the land" (Jeremiah 1:14). Jeremiah surely knows that this vague, unnamed foe from the north refers to the Babylonians. He also understands that if Judah does become a victim, its soon-to-be conquerors and killers (the Babylonian emperor and his army) will merely be acting as God's instruments to punish it for its repeated sins and transgressions.

Speaking as a mouthpiece for God, Jeremiah recounts to his people the love and fidelity that once bound the two together, the intimate partnership that helped carry the Israelites through the harsh wilderness of Sinai and into the Promised Land. That bond and trust were shattered when God's people began to neglect those in need and started to kneel before foreign idols. Now their unfaithfulness will have dire consequences.

Jeremiah presents the evidence for God's indictment of the people of Israel, and there is great anger in his words: "To a land like a garden I brought you, to eat of its bountiful fruit. But you entered and defiled my land, and made my heritage loathsome. . . . So consider and see how bitterly evil it is to have forsaken Adonai your God. . . . A noble vine I planted you, of wholly reliable stock. But what a foul-smelling thing you have become, a strange, wild vine! Though you scrub yourself with lye, and use as much soap as you wish, still the stain of your guilt is before me" (Jeremiah 2:7, 19, 21–22).

At the heart of these images and metaphors is the theme of betrayal. Despite the gifts of land, produce, and, most of all, redemption, the Israelites are charged with flagrant and inexcusable apostasy. Jeremiah delivers this charge and attack on Judah—the final remnant—with stinging allusions. The people of Israel have, through their actions and inactions, irreparably contaminated their sacred inheritance (the "land") as well as themselves. They have forgotten their God, and they have soiled their own souls.

Jeremiah continues: "Where are your gods, which you made for yourself? Let them rise, if they can, and save you in your time of distress. For as numerous as your cities are your gods, O Judah. Why complain to me? You have all rebelled against me. . . . I will bring you to judgment. . . . Egypt will disappoint you, just as Assyria did. You will come away with your hands on your head, for Adonai has spurned those you have trusted. You will discover no success through them" (Jeremiah 2:28–29, 35–37).

As a taunt, the prophet tells Judah to turn to the gods they have worshipped instead of God if they want to escape their fate. He also makes it clear that no alliance with Egypt or Assyria will save them, either. It seems that there is no hope.

Jeremiah offers one last chance, however. Speaking in God's voice, he says: "If you return, O Israel—to me, return—if you put your vile things aside and stray not from my presence, then might you swear 'As Adonai lives,' truthfully, justly, and rightly. Then the nations would bless themselves by [me], and in [me] exult" (Jeremiah 4:1–2).

Although these passages reflect the extent of Adonai's anger with the people of Judah, they also represent a desire, on God's part, for repair and reconciliation. Jeremiah's initial, harsh rebukes are followed by a plea for repentance. A renewed relationship with God is the only path left if the Israelites are to avoid the impending catastrophe. In the end, Judah does not return to God, and conquest, destruction, and exile to Babylonia become its fate. Jeremiah, in his role as divine messenger, uses his rage and righteous indignation as both a stick and a carrot: what he seeks is no more—and no less—than a revitalized, moral, and truly sacred society. Tragically, that transformation doesn't happen. Yet Jeremiah remains a model of the steadfast spiritual warrior, a biblical prophet who utilizes his powerful spirit and "tough love" to fight to the bitter end for his people.

———

While anger has its place and its uses, expressing it openly is risky business, a bit like letting a genie out of a bottle: it can be hard to control, reckless, and at times wayward. If we are not very careful, anger can easily degenerate into hatred. While in certain contexts anger can be warranted and even inspire positive and constructive change, when it gets taken over by hatred, the results are uniformly dangerous and destructive. Hatred is at the core all expressions of extremism: sexism, racism, anti-Semitism, and so many others, especially in the area of religion. Though it didn't achieve its desired outcome, Jeremiah's fury was meant to motivate his people to repair their relationship with God. But the hateful rage of religious extremists is a dark, mutated end in itself, and it can too often lead not to social reforms, but to antisocial atrocities.

Jung viewed this emotion as a distortion, not an acceptance, of our shadow, a warped and irrational perception of reality. If our conscious attention to our shadow emotions is incorrect or misguided, that is when they can become damaging and lead to immorality and even violence. Vigilance is our best defense. Whether our opposition is an entire society or simply someone standing in front of us on the dojo floor, we must never fall prey to hatred. Anger has its role in the life of a spiritual warrior, but it must always be kept in check. We are allowed, even *obligated*, to protest (against injustice) and to protect (ourselves, those we love, and others who cannot defend themselves).

But that is our boundary.

In its soundest and, perhaps, most "religious" manifestation, anger in the form of moral outrage (e.g., Jeremiah confronting the indifference and transgressions among his people, or Jesus overturning the tables of the money changers beside the sacred Temple in Jerusalem) can lead to the betterment of ourselves and our world. If God is our moral anchor, then we, as images of the divine and imitators of the divine nature, should never allow immoral or unjust acts to sit comfortably with us. There is a murky border of which we must be cautious. The rage that can serve as a catalyst for social change or as an expression of spiritual obligation is very different from the rage that can separate us from or cause harm to other people—and, ultimately, rupture our holy covenant with God.

FEAR

We often recoil from, or become angered by, those things in our lives that instill fear in us, whether it is a tough sparring partner, a daunting work project, or a personal illness. Fear is one of those inner demons that, like rage, can take us over and make us act in ways that cause harm to ourselves or others, or paralyze us completely. In light of the very real dangers of our world and our own (mis)perceptions of other people, fear is an aspect of our shadow that we must face—and fight—on an everyday basis.

Sometimes, however, fear crosses over into terror. It can be raw, primal, and as palpable as the sound of brush crunching under a predator's paws.

The summer before I was to move to Jerusalem to begin rabbinical school, I decided to drive alone around Lake Michigan, making a loop from my parents' home in Chicago. I wanted to visit some close friends who lived in Madison, Wisconsin, and Ann Arbor, Michigan, but the highlight of my modest road trip would be exploring Michigan's remote Upper Peninsula. I'd always heard about how rugged and beautiful the region was, and I figured I'd do some very physical backpacking and hiking through it as a sort of "boot camp" for the far more *meta*physical rigors of my upcoming religious training.

The Porcupine Mountains sit just across the northwestern border with Wisconsin. The "Porkies," as these ragged midwestern ranges and ridges are commonly known, were named by the native Ojibwa people, supposedly because their undulating, irregular silhouette resembled the shape of a porcupine. They comprise Michigan's largest area of undeveloped wilderness and serve as the home to brawling mountain rivers, high lakes, and dark, old-growth forests, including the largest stand of virgin hardwood hemlock trees in the entire United States. The wildlife in the park there is varied and plentiful, and it contains an especially large, active population of black bears.

My plan was to hike several miles into the park along backcountry trails to see the spectacular Lake of the Clouds, make camp near another stunning location, Mirror Lake, and then hike back out the next day. It would be a quick overnight jaunt. There was a lot that I still wanted to see in the Upper Penninsula—other state parks, old copper mining towns, fishing villages farther north along Lake Superior—and my time was limited.

After checking in with the park ranger, I hauled out the gear from the trunk of my car (a black Dodge Shadow): my backpack and sleeping bag, a tent and rain tarp, some food and water, a small "bear-proof" container, nylon rope, and a well-used commando knife that had always come in handy for me on previous camping trips.

A few hours later, I reached an overview of Lake of the Clouds, and it was indeed spectacular. I sat on a boulder and lunched while gazing at the shimmering mountain lake before me. I struggled to stay in the moment, to simply *be* as my mind raced ahead to thoughts of Jerusalem, to graduate school, and to other distractions that dragged me away from the present. At this point in my inner journey, particularly following my experience in the Tombs, I didn't even try to fight anymore.

I just hiked on.

Mirror Lake came into view toward the end of the day. The forest around it was lush and the trees were tall; with limited sunlight below for small plants and shrubs to grow, it was easy to find a clear, smooth spot on the ground where I could make camp. I set up my tent and tarp, ate dinner by the lake, brushed my teeth, and then placed the rest of my food and any other odor-producing items (even the toothpaste) inside my bear-proof canister, which I hung between two trees with some nylon rope I'd cut.

By then it was dusk, and the forest floor was darkening fast. I entered and zipped up the tent, crawled into my sleeping bag, and did some writing in my journal.

Some time passed. I was tired, and it was getting hard to keep my eyes open, let alone write. I put down my pen and got ready to go to sleep.

Suddenly, I heard what sounded like footsteps heading toward my tent.

"Hey!" I called out. There was no response.

"Who's there?" Again, silence.

The steps got heavier and more pronounced.

If it had been a man out there, surely he would have said something by now. But my words were met by nothing at all. The steps got closer. I grew anxious.

Just then, I heard a second set of steps start to approach me from a different direction. There were two living beings—unseen and unknown—within feet of me, and all that separated us was a thin sheet of fabric. My anxiety morphed into fear.

It was only after these beings encircled me, making sniffing noises louder than any I'd ever heard from a dog, that I reached for my knife. I unlocked the blade.

Though I suspected what they were, I needed to know for sure. There was a flap in the back of my tent. As I slowly unzipped it, I could discern the vague outline of a bear through the murky dusk. It just stood there. Then a second one came into view.

Two mature black bears were trying to get into my tent. They were clearly searching for food. That front zipper was the only thing keeping them out, and I imagined a worst-case scenario: what if they clawed through the fabric and climbed into the tent—and on top of me? I estimated that these bears were probably two or three hundred pounds each. I'd be helpless. Though I didn't want to harm them, I didn't want to die, either. I was ready to plunge that blade into their sides, hoping to hurt them enough that they'd figure I was more trouble than I was worth and move on somewhere else.

"Go away!" I shouted. "Leave me alone! Get out of here!"

As if the bears understood English.

I swore, I gripped the commando knife, and I was filled with a raw, elemental terror. But after several more minutes of my shouting, and their sniffing and shuffling around my tent—and at moments we were only inches apart from each other—the bears stopped their activity. I could hear them silently slink away into the early evening.

They were done with me.

While, in hindsight, I realize that banging my hiking boots together very loudly might have been more effective than a commando knife to someone in my situation, my fear was still very real. Yet as it began to dissipate, and as I was alone with my thoughts until the next morning, I came to view those bears more as teachers than as adversaries. During my harrowing moments with them, there was no psychic room for ruminations about Jerusalem, graduate school, or anything else. All I could experience was a fundamental, all-consuming sense of self. I was no warrior, but I had been brought face-to-face with yet another aspect of my shadow, the most primitive aspect of my being. I understood just how badly I wanted to live—and I saw just how terribly afraid I was to die.

That was progress on the spiritual path.

SMOKE AND MIRRORS

What do we do when we find ourselves standing toe-to-toe with someone, or some thing, more overtly "powerful" than ourselves? This question is applicable not only when we encounter wild animals or confront martial arts opponents, but also when we go through the pain and turbulence of a divorce, the grief over losing a parent, or the heartfelt struggle about our belief in God. Uncertainty can lead to intimidation, intimidation to doubt, and doubt to fear. But when we face our fear, we can learn a great deal from it, and, over time, even surmount it. One thing we can learn is that our perceptions of life do not reliably disclose its realities.

In "The Tyger," William Blake writes:

> Tyger Tyger burning bright,
> In the forests of the night:
> What immortal hand or eye,
> Dare frame thy fearful symmetry?

As Blake seems to express through the verses of this poem (and as I experienced with the bears in the Upper Peninsula), the fact that such a wondrous and frightening creature exists at all can be thought provoking, even transformational—but only if we view it through the right lens and with the proper perspective. Blake's question is fundamental: what *other* sort of being could possibly possess the creativity—and capability—to produce such a marvel of flesh and blood? The tiger, in this respect, is revelatory, a living testimony to the transcendent force that created it. Rather than a work of art, it is a mark of divinity. Our fear of this powerful and mysterious animal is, at a more profound level, simply a veil for our awe of God.

We just don't always recognize it.

Many mystics hold similar views. Rabbi Yaakov Yosef of Polonnoye, one of the first (and most prolific) Hasidic thinkers and theorizers from the late eighteenth century, writes that "the mouse fears the cat, and the cat fears the dog, and likewise the kid [fears] the wolf, and the wolf the lion, and [so on with] the rest of the predatory animals. The same [phenomenon] is true with human beings—the weaker fears the stronger. And the fear of the king is felt by all human beings, [and so on] until the highest point, which is the Root of every fear, as it is written, 'What does the Lord your God require of you, but to fear the Lord your God?' (Deuteronomy 10:12)."

The great twelfth-century rabbi and rationalist philosopher

Moses Maimonides claimed that fear and awe were not just the products of our instinctive, subjective reactions. He argued that when we reflect deeply on the world—in its fullness and totality, with its varied and complex arrangement of beings and experiences—we can't help but respond with these emotions. Maimonides writes that fear and trembling are the logical reactions to the awareness of our small place in the cosmos, and to the limited and finite knowledge we possess in relation to the infinite knowledge of our Creator. It is this realization of our humanity compared with God's divinity that results in these disconcerting feelings. Yet that unease can serve as a portal, helping to break down our defenses and allowing the transcendent to find entry into our souls.

The path of inner growth and self-awareness isn't an easy one, and it can, at times, seem paradoxical. It can take a very jarring event, something primal and even primitive, to catapult us toward more lofty and profound feelings and insights about our lives and the world. But we must recognize that these diverse, at times discomforting experiences are all part of the same spectrum. If we work to develop the tools to see *through* them, though, then our baser fears can awaken us to the reality of, and reverence for, the transcendent—and enrich, elevate, and empower us in the process.

Whatever we may think we fear, the real source of our dread is ultimately our own humanity, our inability to control our fate, our finitude in the face of God's infinity. And if we are ready, if we are evolved internally, we can use that to our benefit. A bold spirituality that uses fear as a springboard for growth is not about succumbing to it, but about seeing beyond it. This approach leads to strength, not weakness.

STRUGGLE AND INTROSPECTION

This chapter has explored the shadow dimension of the human personality and the vital role it plays in each of our spiritual journeys. I have focused especially on the experiences of anger and fear—and how we often must struggle with those forces within us if we are to move forward, grow stronger, and mature. Yet struggle *itself* can serve as a critical weapon in our perpetual war to perfect ourselves both inwardly and outwardly (in our relations with others). I have toiled over the years to become the best rabbi, martial artist, author, son, friend, and man that I could possibly be.

And I continue to struggle, to fall short, and to strive to work harder.

Many of history's spiritual warriors have made the concept of struggle an integral component of their own programs for self-transformation. One of Catholicism's greatest and most influential mystics, St. John of the Cross (1542–1591), understood from direct personal experience about the importance of wrestling with inner demons and darkness. John was ordained as a priest at the age of twenty-one after having been raised in poverty in a small Spanish town near Ávila. He later developed a very close relationship with another famous and important Catholic mystic, St. Teresa of Ávila, who at the time was working hard with her Carmelite sisters to bring about reforms in the church.

The church eventually grew less tolerant of these reformers, and the political situation toward them became hostile—the era's religious authorities viewed Teresa, John, and their spiritual compatriots as rebels and agitators. John was denounced to the Inquisition, and on the night of 1577, he was kidnapped by a band of friars and forcibly imprisoned for the next nine months in a monastery in Toledo as punishment for his actions and activism. It was in a dark, tiny cell that John was repeatedly beaten by his more "obedient" Carmelite brothers, and where he likely had to wrestle with the dark forces (such as anger, fear, loneliness, and doubt) within his own soul as well.

John composed poems in his head about his inner struggle, probably in part as a way to stay sane and mentally strong. That strength surely must have helped him when he made a daring, dramatic escape from the monastery by tying together strips of cloth taken from his blanket and shirt and lowering himself down a high wall from his window.

In the years that followed, John of the Cross wrote down those poems. The greatest among them is "The Dark Night of the Soul," a poem—and a spiritual pathway—in which darkness, and our struggle with it, is not just a background image but the very means by which a human being grows and ultimately encounters God.

Two centuries after John of the Cross, a very significant Jewish mystic, the Hasidic master Rabbi Shneur Zalman of Lyady (1745–1813), had a similar experience of betrayal, imprisonment, and struggle with the dark night. Shneur Zalman was born in Belorussia and began his Jewish studies—with their traditional focus on the Torah, the Talmud, and rabbinic legal codes—at a very early age. Though he was a child prodigy who demonstrated tremendous intellectual gifts, Shneur Zalman believed that something was missing, and he experienced a deep inner yearning and restlessness. The young student felt that his heart had to catch up with his brain, that while he had learned to serve God through reason, he had not developed the capacity to serve God with his soul.

Shneur Zalman left the world of the yeshiva and joined the nascent, decidedly nonmainstream Hasidic movement, where he received intensive instruction in the Kabbalah and was exposed to dynamic practices and new, sometimes radical ideas. Very soon he became an important and fresh voice in the movement himself, ultimately creating his own Hasidic system and dynasty, known today as Chabad-Lubavitch.

The traditional rabbinic establishment (referred to as the Mitnagdim, "Those who stand in opposition") had never been comfortable with Hasidism's mystical approach to Judaism, and they felt increasingly threatened by this new movement's growing popularity. Another serious problem was a "brain drain"— religious schools and synagogues were losing some of their best and brightest young scholars and future leaders (such as Shneur

Zalman), who were more attracted to Hasidism than they were to conventional study and worship. By the late eighteenth century, this conflict between the Hasidim and the Mitnagdim intensified. The enormous rise of Hasidism among the Jewish masses had become a grave threat to rabbinic dominance, and Hasidism itself was attacked as anti-intellectual and, by some authorities, as heretical. Shneur Zalman, who was now seen as one of Hasidism's central figures, caused concern and antipathy.

Just as several of John of the Cross's own Carmelite brothers kidnapped him because of his reformist views, some of Shneur Zalman's fellow rabbis engineered a plan to silence him and try to slow the spread of Hasidism. In 1798, the chief rabbi of Pinsk turned informer to the czar, falsely accusing Shneur Zalman of treason against the state (he had made charitable contributions to Palestine, which the rabbi presented as evidence of "helping the Turkish sultan") and of forming a religious sect (since in czarist Russia all sects were prohibited by law). Shneur Zalman was arrested, taken to St. Petersburg to stand trial, and convicted. He spent time in prison, but was later acquitted and freed. Three years later, though, he was arrested again on the same charges and was imprisoned once more.

Much in the spiritual life and literary work of Shneur Zalman appeared to take a new direction following his experiences in prison. He became more inner directed, more open, and unusually accepting of the terrible things that had been done to him. In his writings, he describes his periods of confinement as the result of divine displeasure with his abilities as a teacher of Hasidism and as signs that he needed to work even harder; he places no blame on others, he expresses no resentment or regret. In his masterwork, the *Tanya*, Shneur Zalman argues that every painful experience, even if its cause is a human agent, is in some way linked to God, the source of everything. What appears to us as evil is, in reality, a masked form of good. Like a pointillist painting whose chaotic dot scheme becomes orderly and beautiful only when viewed from a proper distance, those struggles and challenges that seem random and repellent to us as they are occurring are essential parts of a purposeful, sacred harmony when seen from a mystical vantage point. There is no such thing as evil—there is only God.

Shneur Zalman saw his time in prison, and the tribulations he underwent there, as a revelation into his own inadequacies, a tool he could use for his own growth.

The path of the spiritual warrior begins by opening ourselves up. But that is only our first step. What we must do next is look inside—and there is no guarantee that we'll like what we actually find. Yet we must contend with it, for our own sake.

The emotions and thoughts that were unleashed for me by my experiences both in the Tombs and with the black bears gave me a taste of what I would later learn from biblical figures, sages, and mystics: something happens to us when we encounter, and struggle with, our shadow side, which can often feel like a prison of our own making (because of the paralyzing effect it can have on us). We become more attuned to our external constraints, more aware of our inner limitations, more eager for and receptive to a world beyond the walls of rage and fear that can confine and cripple our souls.

How we grow from this struggle depends on who we are as individuals, on our psychological makeup, and on personal circumstances. If we are open to its transformative power, doing battle with the darkness within us can lead to deeper, richer lives and reshape forever the way we perceive ourselves and the human condition.

There is a Kabbalistic concept called *yeridah lifney ha-aliyah*, or descent before ascent. For many Jewish mystics, a turbulent plunge into the abyss is viewed as a kind of sacred pilgrimage, a trial through which our souls are tested and refined. The struggle that accompanies this difficult descent is an inevitable and necessary experience in the life of a searching, thoughtful person. It doesn't have to be as dramatic as some of the experiences illustrated in this chapter, but it usually does have a concrete context.

As we learned in the introduction, the Gaon of Vilna points out that although the human soul has a tripartite structure (NaRaN), it is only at the middle level of ruach, or spirit, that we duel with our demons. For him, the story of the biblical prophet Jonah represents the quintessential allegory of a soul's journey from descent and death to ascent and renewed life. Unlike the prophets before him, Jonah rejects God's call. Instead, he flees "down" to the port of Jaffa and "down" into the hold of a ship. During a sudden storm, he is tossed over the vessel's side and descends still further, "down" into the wine-dark waves and "down" into the belly of a sea monster. Clearly, the repetition of these words and images is intended to demonstrate the depth of Jonah's spiritual freefall.

Yet it is while the prophet starts to drown in the straits of his own imprisonment that he finds liberation. Jonah comes to recognize that it was his fear of the prophetic call (his mission was to excoriate the sinful city of Nineveh) that brought him to this dismal, desperate place. This insight frees him to go forward, and he expresses gratitude to God for his newfound perspective, determination, and strength: "From the belly of Sheol [the netherworld] I cried, and you heard my voice. . . . I will look again at your holy Temple. . . . You brought up my life from the pit, Adonai my God. . . . With a thankful voice I will make an offering to you; what I have vowed I will fulfill" (Jonah 2:1, 4, 6, 9).

To the Gaon, the great fish in which Jonah experiences his epiphany and transformation is a symbol for the angel Dumah, ruler of the underworld. Hearkening to the prophet's heartfelt words, God compels Dumah to spit out Jonah, and he lands safely on dry land in order to carry out his original charge. In Jonah's case, as so often in ours—whether we are terrified by death, caught in the thick of a nasty divorce, or paralyzed by an addiction—life can sometimes feel like a pit from which there is no escape. The message of this tale, however, is that descent is often the preparation for our ascent.

Beyond the uncertainty and pain of our encounters with darkness is the light of redemption. When we despair and lose hope, when we give up rather than embrace our struggles, then *we* become our own worst enemies. Our challenge is to draw the spiritual lessons from our brushes with the abyss and allow them to inform—and *trans*form—our lives. If we truly believe that we can learn from our struggles, that they can ultimately make us stronger, we will expand our souls and take another step ahead on the path of inner development. We need to brave our dark nights and brace for the coming dawn.

3

IMMERSE YOURSELF

ONCE WE HAVE GROWN more comfortable with—and learned the virtues of—our vulnerability, and after we have come to terms with (or slain the unhealthy aspects of) our shadow side, we now have a solid foundation from which to continue our journeys toward self-improvement and self-empowerment. This is the time when immersion, patience, and discipline play such a vital role in the life of the spiritual warrior, the time when we must hold up a mirror to ourselves, whatever our particular faith or tradition, and see where we are in relation to where we are urged, and in some instances required, to be. This is the moment when we have to get down to serious business.

IMMERSION AS A TOOL FOR SELF-KNOWLEDGE

I recall one experience vividly, and more than any other, when all three of the elements above were tightly interwoven in a way that I have never forgotten.

It was midnight, and a full moon illuminated a large, grassy field on the campus of Hampshire College in Massachusetts. In absolute silence, save for the sound of bare feet moving through wet grass, a sea of murky human figures seemed to glide back and forth, striking with their fists into nothingness. I was part of that sea. Dressed in our white *gis,* we looked like a gathering of ghosts as we did our training.

Our practice that night was to perform precisely one thousand *oizukis,* or front punches. The task for each of us was to try to make just one of them perfectly. Yet as I judged each and every *oizuki* I made, I would inevitably catch a mistake of some sort—my fist wasn't tight enough, I'd lifted my back heel, my hips weren't thrust forward. We would later learn from our senior instructors that even the greatest of the karate masters acknowledged to their students that they had never achieved what seemed so basic an objective in their entire lifetimes, in *any* of their techniques. It was a task with no end.

That experience was part of an annual retreat, unique in the martial arts world, known as "special training." During special training, which usually involves over a hundred participants, you eat, drink, and breathe karate for five consecutive days. It is an experience of total immersion. Other than your meals and the few hours of sleep you receive each night, all you do is train.

Most days of that special training at Hampshire College involved four practice sessions, each focused on a different aspect of our training (e.g., punches, blocks, kicks). The sessions were highly intense and very difficult—everybody pushed themselves to their limits. That was the purpose. Some fainted, some got sick, some gave up and simply drove home. By the end of those five days, everyone had grown exponentially in their own karate skills. Much of it was related to the constant repetition, the discipline, the singularity of focus, and the energy that we drew from one another. I always felt that my level of ability spiked noticeably following a special training retreat. And I always grew more aware of how much further I had to strive to achieve "perfection."

There are important and striking parallels in the teachings of the spiritual warrior I discussed in the first chapter, Resh Lakish. He states in the Talmud: "If you see a student for whom his studies are as hard as iron, it is because he has failed to systematize them, as it is said, 'he is like one who does not whet the edge [of his blade].' What is the student's remedy? Let him attend to his studies on a more regular basis."

This passage relates to the themes of this chapter—and the third principle in our program of inner development—in many ways. What happens to swordsmen who never sharpen their swords? The same thing that happens to baseball players who skip batting practice or actors who miss rehearsal—they get rusty, they make mistakes, and their work becomes much more difficult. It is only through discipline and repetition that we can avoid these problems. The more regular and systematized our training is, the better we will become in our field and the easier our work will feel.

According to the Talmud, "Resh Lakish made it his practice to repeat in systematic order his lessons forty times, corresponding to the forty days during which Scripture was given. Only then would he come before his master."

In order to stay sharp as a religious student and teacher, Resh Lakish created a private training technique, based on the story of how the Torah was revealed at Mount Sinai, that allowed him to learn more effectively. Before he would ever approach one of his own teachers to demonstrate any advances in his knowledge, Resh Lakish would go over his lessons, again and again, until he was certain he was ready.

He was in no hurry to "reveal" a thing.

A common refrain among those who watch world-class athletes or musicians (to highlight only two examples from many other fields with elite practitioners) is that "they make it look so easy!" What these spectators may not fully appreciate is the devotion and regularity of the individual training that precedes the public presentation. Whatever the field, the people who are the most exceptional in it are invariably the ones who are most deeply immersed in their disciplines—and the most passionate about them.

IMMERSION AS A TOOL FOR TRANSFORMATION

During my first year of rabbinical school, I lived in Kiryat Shmuel, a beautiful neighborhood in Jerusalem. Every Friday afternoon, my routine was the same: I'd buy food for Shabbat in the local markets, go to rugby practice at the Givat Ram stadium of Hebrew University, and then clean up for services. There were many synagogues near my apartment, and almost each week I'd try out a new one with friends.

Several of the synagogues had a *mikveh* (ritual bath) attached to them. I'd been in a mikveh only once before, an unusual one that had been built into the cleft of a mountain in the Galilee, while I was a college student in Israel three years before. It had been a very powerful experience, but it had never occurred to me that ritual immersion would ever become a regular part of my religious and spiritual life—especially of my Shabbat preparation. Taking a shower after rugby practice paled in comparison.

There was a mikveh down the street from my apartment, in the basement of a synagogue named Yad Tamar, that I particularly liked. Though I was invariably viewed by the other bathers with a degree of suspicion (since I did not look the part of the typical ultra-Orthodox mikveh user), I always looked forward to my weekly immersion. Shabbat started to seem somehow different, somehow purer—or perhaps *I* was the one who had changed. My commitment to that ritual, the constancy of my observance to it, afforded me both a challenge and a steady source of comfort.

When I moved back to the United States to continue my rabbinical studies, it became too difficult to go to a mikveh every Friday; there just weren't enough of them close to me. And, to be totally honest, I had probably grown lazy. But I longed for that neighborhood mikveh, so I tried to bathe myself each week in its memory—as well as in my memories of Jerusalem—instead of its waters.

In classical Jewish writings, the waters of a mikveh are referred to as *mayim chayim*, or living waters. It is essential that they come from a natural source, such as a spring, stream, or rainwater, and they must completely envelop the person who enters them. Not even the hair on your head should float above the surface. It was just this feature—the idea of envelopment, of engulfment—that made going to the mikveh such a meaningful, and at times transcendent, experience for me. As many Jews wrap prayer shawls around their shoulders before they begin to worship, so do the waters of the mikveh wrap themselves around our bodies as we descend the steps of its pool.

The mikveh, both in intention and in imagery, is about transformation and transportation. As Rabbi Aryeh Kaplan explains the practice in *Waters of Eden* (an extensive modern commentary and meditation on this ancient ritual), while the water of a mikveh purifies our bodies, the divine presence that resides in it purifies our soul: "Everything in the physical world has a spiritual counterpart. Every action in this world likewise has its counterpart in the spiritual realm. The spiritual counterpart of a physical man is his divine soul. When a man immerses in a physical mikveh, his soul likewise becomes immersed in its own spiritual counterpart."

The ritual of water immersion represents our entrance into an utterly different medium, one that surrounds us on all sides. This can be seen as symbolizing our entrance into a new state of consciousness, where God's presence is revealed. Taking the symbolism even further, we can view immersion in a mikveh as an immersion in the waters of wisdom, whereby *all* reality reveals God's presence. According to Rabbi Asher of Stolin, a nineteenth-century Hasidic master, "Through [the ritual of the] mikveh you can come to unity. For mikveh immersion points to the truth, that there is no place where God is not—for the water completely surrounds you."

Water immersion, when viewed through a metaphysical lens, has the capacity to change both our souls and our perception of the world around us. When we observe this ritual practice, we can transform ourselves in potent and palpable ways. I have never stepped out of a mikveh without feeling genuinely different—

calmer, clearer, and more grounded. Many thinkers, recognizing the ability of the mikveh to effect this dramatic kind of an experience in human beings, offer some fascinating interpretations of the ritual related to renewal and rebirth, death and resurrection.

In Kaplan's words, "The mikveh represents the womb. When an individual enters the mikveh, he is re-entering the womb, and when he emerges, he is as if born anew." But this isn't any womb—it is the *divine* womb. When fully immersed, naked and enveloped by liquid, we are like a fetus in the womb of its mother, and when we eventually rise up out of the pool of the mikveh, we are reborn. It is as if our old self dies and is resurrected as a different being, like a newborn child (with new hopes, dreams, and possibilities). This death-birth dynamic is captured by another important Hasidic mystic and teacher, the Maggid Ta'alumah: "The intention you should have when you immerse yourself in the mikveh is that, doubled-over, you are like a fetus within its mother, and when you emerge, you are born as a new creation—you have given up your life to God."

This analogy with death is just as significant as that of birth. "When a person immerses himself in water," Kaplan comments, "he places himself in an environment where he cannot live. Were he to remain submerged for more than a few moments, he would die from lack of air. He is thus literally placing himself in a state of non-existence and non-life. Thus, when a person submerges himself in a mikveh, he momentarily enters the realm of the non-living, so that when he emerges he is like one reborn."

It takes courage and a kind of generosity to deliberately enact (and, in a certain sense, rehearse) your own death, but self-transformation only comes through self-sacrifice. That is why this ancient ritual is so consonant with the attitude and spirit of the true warrior. And when it is performed in a disciplined way and on a regular basis, it affords us with the opportunity of becoming "a new creation," a more evolved human being ready to take on life's challenges and receptive to the power of practice.

GEARING UP

You don't need an actual mikveh to attain the phenomenon of deep inner transformation. You need only immerse yourself in working on your soul. Genuine immersion requires many things, but it is impossible without discipline and repetition. We need to train, to practice, to find the right teachers and traditions that fit our desires and objectives. But we also need to utilize the proper tools, or weapons, to enhance this process and to help with our development as potential spiritual warriors.

We need to gear up.

This "gear" can come in a wide-ranging variety of forms and/ or expressions (material objects, actions, observances), but it is always ritualistic in the ways that we harness it in our training. In fact, it *is* ritual. Whether making forward thrust strikes with a *bo* staff or covering our heads with a prayer shawl during certain moments in a worship service, ritual is at the very core of any area we want to develop.

Why do I wear a *kippah* (the skullcap more commonly known by its Yiddish name, yarmulke) when I pray, but not on the street? For me, putting on a kippah before entering a synagogue is like donning a *gi* before walking onto the floor of a dojo. Both of these ritual objects serve a vital function—they help me, in a palpable, tactile way, to separate the mundane from the metaphysical, the ordinary from the spiritual. I use a kippah and a gi to help me with my journeys through the traditions of my faith and of karate.

Rituals have been a part of human civilization for millennia, and they are not limited to the world of organized religion. Partly because of their primeval roots, I find I gain a wonderful feeling of *comfort* whenever I utilize them. When I perform the precise and ritualized movements of a kata, it is as if I am wrapping myself in a protective cloak that has been worn by other practitioners for centuries. Whatever moves (or missteps) I might make during the practice of a particular form have most assuredly been made by countless other students long before I ever arrived on the martial arts scene. When I utter certain Hebrew prayers during services, I am reciting the same words that have flowed from the mouths of my parents, grandparents, and forebears for thousands of years. In either case, the "gear" I use conveys to me the sense that I am not alone.

It guides me, it supports me, and it spurs me on.

Every tradition meant to enrich and improve our lives has its own set of rituals. Often there are similarities, as when I bow both before the open ark of a synagogue and prior to engaging with a training partner in a dojo. Yet physical and spiritual immersion is the key to all of them. In Jewish practice, I wrap the black leather straps and box of my tefillin (prayer phylacteries) in a very specific sequence and way around my left arm, hand, and even fingers, and only then affix the other straps and box to my head. *How* I put on tefillin is as ritualistic in nature as are the ritual objects themselves.

Although tefillin are meant, traditionally, to be worn by Jews in preparation for morning worship services, I sometimes feel when I am putting them on as if I am gearing up for some kind of battle. And maybe that's what the rabbinic masters really intended all along—to create rituals to help us train and protect our souls.

The same ideas relate to the realm of martial arts. When I use an object, such as a *makiwara* (straw-padded striking post), in order to condition my fists, or when I bow before a photo of Master Funakoshi before practice, I am utilizing traditional rituals in order to train and direct my body and mind. A kata may not be a physical object, but it is certainly a martial arts ritual, and when I immerse myself in its movements, it becomes an intimate and important source of comfort, motivation, and strength.

According to Master Funakoshi, the purpose of learning kata is "for the tempering and disciplining of oneself." He goes on: "Do not expect good results in a short time. Karate training may extend over one's entire life. In the study of any subject, little is to be gained from haphazard training, and thus, particularly in a martial art such as karate, steady, unremitting training is required. Train systematically, without becoming impatient or overexerting yourself, and develop gradually, advancing steadily, one step at a time, with increased application of force and numbers of exercises practiced."

A warrior of the spirit understands—and embraces—this foundational idea. Envelop yourself, not only in teachings and techniques, but in patience.

When I perform a karate form such as Bassai ("To Penetrate a Fortress") or Kwanku ("To Look at the Sky"), I am using the swift and powerful movements of the kata not just to develop my mind, body, and spirit, but also to honor and perpetuate (and strive to perfect) the expression of a ritual. Like the fixed dance sequences in a ballet, the many, varied, and majestic kata constitute the heart and soul of the art itself.

Without ritual—whether it takes the form of a material object, words, or an ordered sequence of physical motions—no spiritual pathway, religious or otherwise, is truly authentic or complete. And, on a practical level, it just won't work. It will be little more than an empty vessel, an inchoate system of goals and ideals that fails to provide its followers with the proper tools necessary for us to realize them.

PATIENCE AND PROGRESSION

The goal of this book is to help transform our souls and strengthen our relationships with the divine. One way of making that challenging objective more likely is by bucking the prevailing trends of our culture and seeking out true anchors from authentic, time-tested traditions and systems. People today want quick fixes and magic bullets. Look at the commercial success of places such as the Kabbalah Center, where students who don't know the difference between the Torah and the Talmud are exposed to the profundities of Jewish mysticism long before they're ready. Or look at martial arts schools where you can walk out the dojo door with a black belt in no more than a year or two—

for the right fee. What is far more important than a quick door-way to the final goal, in addition to immersive and disciplined practice, is to first have a solid background in the *fundamentals*. How is this idea supported by other fields and by history? Think about the arts. As I illustrated in my book *Gonzo Judaism*, Pablo Picasso learned how to draw conventional human figures long *before* his bold experiment with Cubism. Miles Davis trained in classical music *prior* to his daring journey into new and revolutionary forms of jazz. It wasn't until both of these great artists had the basics of their respective genres down cold that they ventured out into uncharted territory.

The bravest and freest of spirits have nearly always been well-rooted ones—at least until they're really ready to fly.

While I have studied the martial arts for fifteen years, it is only because I have a strong foundation (a black belt in karate) that I now feel free to try out other styles, such as tae kwon do and boxing. This applies to the spiritual arena as well. You won't ever be able to perform a reverse hook kick—or experience divine communion—until you begin your journey by first learning how to stand, strike, breathe . . . or pray.

In an era when so many of us want to find the fastest road to success, this steady commitment to learning the fundamentals isn't an easy task or the best marketing strategy—but it's the correct path to follow. Yet one of the gravest failings of modernity is its inability to tolerate this hard-to-swallow reality. Our consumerist culture is much more comfortable when it proclaims:

I know what I want, and I want it ASAP.

I don't have the time to work for it—I'll just buy this popular self-help book from a guy I saw on afternoon television and skim through it this weekend.

There is nothing that is beyond my reach.

For better or worse, some things *are* beyond our reach—at the start. When we look for shortcuts, when we skip challenging but essential steps in our development, we are doing ourselves a serious disservice. Whether it is in the field of dieting or finding a more spiritual life, we must begin the process by learning basic principles and practices if we are to experience anything in its deepest and most meaningful expression.

It is crystal clear to anyone who has ever studied the Kabbalah, for instance, that it is impossible to truly grasp or appreciate the beauty and majesty of this esoteric mystical tradition unless we first have a rudimentary knowledge of Judaism itself—the anchor and foundation from which Kabbalah, and all of Jewish mysticism, emerges. When a group like the Kabbalah Center skips that step (in an effort to increase its number of students, as well as its bank account) it can lead to far more harm than good.

It's somewhat analogous to a martial arts instructor who awards someone a black belt too early into training. That unfortunate student might start to swagger down the street with a wonderful feeling of accomplishment and strength, but all the teacher has really done is given that person a false and artificial sense of confidence and security, leaving him or her dangerously unprepared in the face of a true confrontation. When our teachers permit us to think that we know more than we actually do or that we've achieved more than we actually have, we enter a fantasy world that ultimately benefits no one and that potentially can be detrimental to our own well-being.

Abraham Maslow, the renowned psychologist, observed that human beings have a hierarchy of needs, a sort of ascending ladder from the most basic (food, sleep, sex) to the most highly evolved (love, wisdom, fulfillment) that we must follow in a specific *progression* if we're to work our way toward the top rung of self-actualization. I would add to Maslow's important observation that we also have a hierarchy of knowledge, including spiritual knowledge. Who would want to be treated by a neurosurgeon who had never taken biochemistry 101 in medical school? And who would turn for religious guidance to a cleric who knew all about mysticism but who couldn't instruct us about the Bible, conduct a worship service, or officiate at a funeral?

This progression idea also applies to us as learners.

When we try to sidestep the fundamentals, all we do is build a house of cards—something without a foundation that is sound only in appearance. It might look nice, but even a gentle breeze would collapse the entire structure.

So how do we learn the basics? The first and probably hardest step is to admit our ignorance. Honesty and humility are virtues, and they are qualities that will give us the strength and fortitude to start the difficult work that is involved as we strive to acquire real knowledge. After we have humbled ourselves and acknowledged that we just can't go it alone if we genuinely want to transform and empower our souls, the next logical step is to reach out to others for help. Judaism's ancient guidebook *Pirke Avot* ("The Sayings of the Fathers") offers two invaluable lessons on this subject: "Do not separate yourself from the community," and, "Find yourself a teacher."

These are lessons that any spiritual seeker needs—not just to hear, but to heed.

It is the first teaching—linking ourselves with a community—that is the biggest obstacle for many of us. We live in an extremely individualistic culture, one that tells us that we don't need to rely on anybody or anything to achieve our personal goals. The historical figures of Jack London, Amelia Earhart, and Jack Kerouac are just a few examples of the "rugged American individualist" so mythologized by our society. My own experience has shown me how enticing separation and solitude can be. As the rabbi of a congregation that at times can be quite demanding of me (and of my time and space), you better believe I know the temptation to withdraw or take flight all too well. Yet I have learned that what takes real strength, and what is ultimately more enriching and transformational, is ongoing, dynamic interaction with other human beings.

Engagement, not evasion, is a mark of the true warrior.

We must act in ways that are counter to the culture we find ourselves in. We must get over our baggage about joining a group—any group—made up of fellow seekers. Whether it is a school or a shul, a dojo or a house of worship, we need the support of others. And then we need to pay our dues—figuratively *and* literally. If we are supported in our efforts, it is only right that we offer support in return. "Love your neighbor," the Bible tells us. If actual love is too tall an order, then at least show some respect.

That's step one. Yet what about the second lesson, the charge to find yourself a teacher? As the member of a community, you are no longer clueless and alone, but exploring your inner self in the company of others. All congregations, martial arts schools, and other institutions devoted to personal and spiritual development have (and are often led by) teachers. The job of these instructors, whether they are professionals or volunteers, is to help us become better at whatever it is that we are working on— our bodies, our minds, or our souls.

Finding the right teacher isn't easy. Different teachers have different personalities, as well as different strengths and weaknesses, and we must have the patience to search out the one (or ones) who is (or are) right for us. Some of these teacher-trainers will be called Sensei or Sifu, some Rabbi or Pastor, and some simply by their first names. But irrespective of their titles, it is the task of these men and women to educate us in their particular fields. They are more knowledgeable, experienced, and evolved in them than we are. Some are masters at very high levels—they are often teachers of teachers.

We must accept the fact that there is an appropriate hierarchy in training and not try to resist it. That is where the role and value of our humility comes into play.

There are exceptions to this rule. Though rabbis have traditionally been my community's primary teachers and transmitters of Judaism, you can find other types of Jewish educators. Depending on your specific context and stage, what you need may not be a scholar but a *peer,* a fellow learner. In *Gonzo Judaism,* I describe how, in classical Jewish education, a *hevruta* is your pedagogic partner, the person you study, discuss, and debate Jewish texts and ideas with. Your hevruta is the person you learn from as well as teach, the training companion on whom much of your religious knowledge—and, from my perspective, your spiritual development—in a very significant way depends.

A hevruta (which derives from the same Hebrew root letters as *havurah,* or community) is like a sparring partner. The two of you are engaged—mostly on an unconscious level—in an intense and intimate battle to transform and, in the end, transcend yourselves. That is what it means to be a spiritual warrior. Training of this nature and degree is nothing like its "secular" counterpart; you don't just sit down in a comfortable chair and read on your own, alone. You interact, dialogue, debate, and *wrestle*—and none of this would be possible in a vacuum of the self. Through the ancient hevruta method, the roles of student and teacher are in a perpetual state of flux.

The Jewish tradition declares that God is present whenever two people study Torah together. Learning is more than the acquisition of data—it is a sacrament.

Once you have connected with a community and found the right teacher, your warrior journey has just begun. Consider yourself a yellow belt. You have a firm foundation in your particular tradition, you feel more secure, and you're ready. You understand that striving to achieve anything of worth in this world, including spiritual growth, involves humility, patience, discipline, and immersion. You grasp that it is the *process,* not necessarily the final result, that counts. Now the training really begins.

The words of the Sh'ma prayer (from the Jewish liturgy) are meaningful for us when we embark on this path of learning: "Take to heart these instructions with which I charge you this day. Impress them upon your children. Recite them when you stay at home and when you are away, when you lie down and when you rise up" (Deuteronomy 6:6–7). There are no shortcuts. The only path toward attaining a well-anchored, renewed, and genuinely empowered soul is through consistent, ongoing study and practice.

Learning for its own sake (*lishma*) is a Jewish obligation as well as a spiritual virtue. It is the quality of our commitment, not the quantity of our knowledge or experience, that truly defines us. Nevertheless, how diligently we immerse ourselves in our training is a reflection of that commitment. Regular, disciplined study and practice give us the tools that are required to live a fulfilling spiritual life, even as they deepen our devotion. That same learning will also help us to develop the capacity, depending on our characters and receptivity, to open new windows to the realm of the divine.

Communion flows from commitment.

So learn the fundamentals of your tradition. Let things take their natural course and evolve. Try to be patient. And be sure your soul has solid footing before you allow it to it take flight— it will fly higher, it will soar farther, and your aim will be truer.

DISCIPLINE AND ITS OUTER LIMITS

At different times in our lives, our soaring souls may very well carry us to some pretty unusual places. For some, serious commitment, in its more conventional forms and expressions, is simply not engaging enough. They crave something far more extreme, something that skirts the very edge and tests their limits—and that's where asceticism comes into being. Asceticism, and some of the ritual "tools" associated with it, has played a constant, dynamic, and frequently colorful role in the history not only of the world's religions, but also of individual spiritual warriors. The ascetic impulse can be found in most faith traditions. Some of its common practices and techniques include isolation, fasting, sexual abstinence, flights into the wilderness, the denial of certain kinds of food and drink, and, in more radical instances, mortification of the body.

I have experimented with ascetic practices during my own spiritual journey, and they have had a profound impact on my life as a man and a rabbi. Much of what follows is drawn from an entire chapter I devoted to the subject in my book *God at the Edge*.

The underlying motivation for most of these (to many of us, bizarre) rituals is a shared one. Asceticism is an extreme—yet also reasoned—response to a profound tension that exists in every spiritual system: the deep craving of human beings, either as individuals or as groups, to realize an ideal of inner perfection while at the same time facing a flawed self and a fractured world that perpetually undermine that goal. An ascetic tries to transcend those barriers, which is why I view asceticism as a special and unique category among the various types and schools of spiritual warriors.

One ancient model of this sort of warrior is the Nazirite, a member of an elite class of ascetics who lived in biblical times and well into the Second Temple era. The Nazirite distinguished himself from other Israelites through his devotion, for a fixed period, to specific disciplines (enumerated in chapter 6 of the book of Numbers) meant to inculcate ritual and spiritual purity: abstention from wine and other grape products; avoidance of contact with the dead; refusal to cut his hair; and vowing to set his life apart from the rest of his community so as to serve God exclusively. One of the most famous examples of a Nazirite is Samson, the warrior-hero from the book of Judges.

Another model of a Jewish ascetic is the Essene, a member of an insular, enigmatic community of men and women who lived apart from their fellow Israelites in Qumran—a remote and isolated desert region—during a period of great national tumult (from about 200 B.C.E. to 100 C.E.). It was there, among the cliffs and in the caves above the Dead Sea, that the Essenes wrote what are now known as the Dead Sea Scrolls. Many contemporary scholars think that the Essenes were sectarians who had broken away from what they believed was a corrupt and sinful religious establishment in Jerusalem, a place where even the holy Temple had been befouled by wicked forces. The Essenes viewed themselves as an army of spiritual warriors, the "Sons of Light" who would confront and vanquish the powers of darkness and return the world to God's rule. Their messianic view was grounded in asceticism, in a rigidly disciplined way of life and social structure designed to prepare their souls for the apocalyptic battle to come.

In order to defeat the forces of darkness, God's warriors had to be pure of soul, mind, and body. Abstinence, even on a temporary basis, was a key component in their rigorous training regimen. Departing from Judaism's normative practices related to sexuality, celibacy played a significant role in the religious life of the Essene community. Sexual desire, along with the constricting bonds of marriage, was perceived largely as a hindrance to their sole mission: preparation for the End of Days. Ritual observance, study, and communal cohesion were their primary focus. Anything that might distract them from these activities and commitments was shunned, avoided, or eliminated.

Yet this semimonastic group, as the Dead Sea Scrolls themselves imply, was more diverse and complex than it is usually portrayed. The Essenes still saw Judaism as their foundation (despite what they saw as its deep institutional flaws). Some scrolls even suggest cases of marriage, demonstrating at least some fidelity to the Jewish duty to procreate. While their ascetic impulses drove the Essenes, both physically and metaphysically, to the outer limits of ancient Jewish society, it was as Jews—and as Jewish warriors, as "Sons of Light"—that they yearned for Armageddon, the cataclysmic war that never arrived.

Manifestations of asceticism emerged in the non-Jewish arena as well. Not long after the eventual disappearance of the Essenes, zealous hermits from the relatively young Christian religion started to head into the wilderness. These men wanted to detach themselves completely from the pagan cities of their time (the fourth century C.E.) and devote themselves to purely spiritual activities. By fleeing deep into the deserts of Egypt, Palestine, Arabia, and Persia, they hoped that seclusion and solitude would wash away the stains of paganism and help lead them to the personal salvation for which they strived.

Among the first of these desert monks (and this category of spiritual warrior) was St. Anthony. Born to wealthy parents who died while he was a young man, Anthony gave away his family's riches to the poor and attempted to develop an ascetic lifestyle near his town. The distractions around him were great, however, and soon Anthony decided to withdraw totally from society and immerse himself in practice and prayer. Initially, Anthony had himself sealed in several desert caves where, according to legend, he triumphed over a series of temptations and trials by the devil. Though these contests seem more fantasy than fact, I'm sure that a worldly and affluent young man like Anthony had plenty of inner demons to wrestle with while cut off from the comforts and pleasures of his prior home and living alone in the middle of the desert. Yet this "father" of the Desert Fathers (as these men would come to be called) saw his isolation as the best means to free himself from all responsibility—except for prayer and the true pursuit of holiness.

As word of Anthony's compelling story spread, more world-weary men followed his example. By 375, the Desert Fathers had established loosely knit communities of monks in the many deserts of the Nile Valley. While most lived in solitary cells, they did gather at times for trade, for worship, and to seek spiritual counsel and instruction from one another.

Anthony (formal sainthood would come much later in church history) was their model of the ascetic-soldier ideal. Like him, a potential hermit had to be someone mature and reasonably evolved in his faith, humble in attitude, and disconnected from the world in body and mind. The Desert Fathers believed—as did many Jewish ascetics—that the divine will was hidden as well as revealed, so they created additional, and often severe, rules, rites, and rituals for themselves in order to test and refine each of their souls.

Solitude and bodily renunciation were prerequisites for the fundamental purpose of the life of a Desert Father: undisturbed meditation on God's will. Only simple, nonintellectual work, such as weaving baskets out of reeds, was allowed. But problems arose nonetheless. The desert's harsh conditions, and human loneliness, broke the spirits of many, driving some to erratic behavior, even insanity. And the spiritual call to self-denial sometimes warped into the exaltation of suffering and pain. Without effective leadership and proper control mechanisms, asceticism could get twisted into an end in itself rather than a means to one. This clear and growing need for vigilance and tighter organization led directly to the beginning of early Christian monasticism and its various orders.

The teachings of this group were collected in a book titled *Verba Seniorum*, "The Sayings of the Fathers" (the same title as the classic Jewish work noted earlier in the chapter, *Pirke Avot*, which was composed at roughly the same time and in the same region of the world). While the many biographies that were later written about the lives of the Desert Fathers tend to be a bit over the top, full of miraculous tales that make them seem like comic book superheroes instead of real-life spiritual warriors, the *Verba* are straightforward aphorisms and stories on the life of faith that were transmitted orally in Coptic until they were canonized and written down in Latin by the church.

Here is one of my favorite teachings from the *Verba*, attributed to an anonymous elder: "If you see a young monk by his own will climbing up into heaven, take him by the foot and throw him to the ground, because what he is doing is not good for him."

This older, wiser sage clearly understood the importance of having patience—and undergoing lifelong training—as we strive to reach the celestial heights. It isn't healthy for our souls to move too fast or too fervently on our spiritual journeys, and, as we have discussed in this chapter, it won't work. We need the help of others. We need teachers to guide us. We need a community to support us. Progression is the key to practice.

Asceticism is, perhaps, one of the more extreme ways a spiritual seeker might become immersed in his or her training. But the path of the warrior should always lead toward self-transcendence, not self-denigration or self-destruction. Some of the practices and techniques (or spiritual "weapons") of the ascetic can be very effective. For example, I have found fasting, silence, isolation, and dietary restrictions to be valuable tools in my own inner work—they have helped me grow in many ways. But when taken to extremes, these practices can backfire and cause damage. They can sever us from others and distance us from social challenges (such as fighting injustice and protecting the weak).

Discipline, commitment, and immersion are essential to our spiritual growth, but they aren't enough. We need humility and patience as well, and we need to view our training not as an end in itself, but as a means to one, something we must work on over and over. We train in order to *transcend* our training. In truth, we train so we can transcend ourselves.

None of this—allowing ourselves to become vulnerable, facing our inner demons, or immersing ourselves in ongoing, often repetitive practice—is easy. Yet these are the steps we have to take (in their right time, place, and sequence) if we are to push past our limits and enlighten and empower our souls. We must believe. We must have guts.

4

NO GUTS, NO GLORY

NO MATTER HOW hard we work on ourselves—with all our practice, honesty, and openness—we will be little more than empty vessels unless we have a heart that directs us, a deep emotional wellspring that motivates and inspires us on our sometimes harrowing journeys through human life and its ongoing, unexpected challenges.

One of the essential things that distinguishes a military warrior from a spiritual one is their different objectives. The goal of the former is clear and clean—to defeat the enemy on the battlefield (or wherever they may be). But the ultimate goal of the latter is harmony, wholeness, and peace. There is a metaphysical as well as *moral* dimension to the path of the spiritual warrior, a path that is not about "victory," but about diving into the existential muck and mire in order to heed the call to become better human beings and, in turn, to work to better the world around us. This path involves special, often difficult requirements. It is a mission for only the bravest of souls.

The mere development of our abilities, be they internal or external, is not enough. Being a warrior is about *will*, not just skill. What that means is that, under certain circumstances, we may very well be tested on our journeys. And those tests will compel us, if we are truly faithful to ourselves and others, to take concrete action, to summon a courage from within our souls that too many of us are not even aware we possess.

BEYOND KEVLAR

While it may seem a bit ironic, owing to my youthful brush with the law (which I described in the second chapter), today I am the national Jewish chaplain for the Federal Law Enforcement Officers Association, the umbrella organization for all the federal law enforcement agencies in the country (e.g., the FBI, DEA, ATF, U.S. Marshals, and dozens of others). Entering the world of cops and criminals, even as a volunteer, isn't a common career move for a rabbi, but the central mission of law enforcement—the pursuit of justice—fuses perfectly, to me, with a core commandment of my faith. The Bible itself declares: "Justice, justice shall you pursue!" (Deuteronomy 16:20).

The military has understood for millennia the importance of having religious figures among its troops. In the Bible, we see Aaron, the high priest, standing watch over battlefields, and Joshua's own priests blowing rams' horns at the walls of Jericho. For inspiration and guidance, the involvement of spiritual men and women in traumatic, life-and-death situations was treated as essential. The position of law enforcement chaplain, however, is a comparatively recent (and somewhat unconventional) creation. I have counseled distraught agents and officers in bars and discussed marital issues in interrogation rooms. I serve as a confidant to special agents of all faith traditions, and of none. I go wherever I'm needed. My work has taken me from memorial ceremonies at what was left of the Alfred P. Murrah Building in Oklahoma City to participating in the bucket brigades at Ground Zero in the immediate aftermath of the 9/11 terrorist attacks.

One of my challenges as a chaplain is that law enforcement officers can be an understandably cynical population to interact with. They face society's dark side on an everyday basis and often have a dim view of the world and humanity. Developing doubts about God's reality, and even about hope itself, are risks that come with the job.

A few years ago, I joined a group of special agents from the Drug Enforcement Administration for a kind of field trip one Sunday morning to Camp Smith, a small base just north of New York City that is used by both the military and law enforcement for training purposes. For the agents, the outing was a mandatory part of their work: they had to go through the process of weapons recertification every year in order to legally carry specific firearms related to their particular area of responsibility (drug trafficking, selling and distribution, organized crime, SWAT, and the like). I was invited—after receiving proper instruction from the weapons masters who were assigned there—to join them on the range, and for the next couple of hours all I could hear was the cacophony of bullets as we fired our Glocks and semiautomatics (from various distances and at different rates of rapidity) at our respective paper targets, the blackened silhouettes of male torsos.

While taking the event seriously, the agents still liked to include a recreational component in the day, so several of them started cooking up hamburgers and hot dogs on a large grill as soon as we'd all finished shooting. I knew most of the agents from the large Manhattan field office, but there were a few others present that day from different areas whom I'd never met before. Over lunch, I caught up with my friends from the city, then introduced myself to the agents I didn't know. One of them, a short, quiet Hispanic man in his forties, sat alone on the grass. I approached and asked if I could join him.

When he discovered that I was a chaplain, the agent seemed intrigued, almost puzzled. "You know, I'm a Catholic," he said.

"Good for you," I answered. "Some of my best friends are Catholic."

He laughed. We spoke for well over an hour, and he was

fascinated by my decision to enter the rabbinate, and even more curious as to why I would want to work with law enforcement agents as part of my vocation.

"It's all about the perks," I said. "This is the only congregation I know of where a government-issued SUV can serve as a pulpit. I'm wearing jeans and I've been shooting guns all day. You can't make this stuff up, my friend."

I asked him to tell me a little about himself. A former Army Ranger, he said that he'd been with the DEA for almost twenty years. He'd worked in several different departments, but most of what he did was undercover surveillance and operations. Because he spoke fluent Spanish, he was often recruited by his supervisors to do urban gang work. "I didn't really like it, but you gotta do what your boss tells you to do."

He said he'd had a few "close calls." I didn't ask him what he currently did.

After some time passed, he shared something else with me: "You know, probably both the highest *and* lowest point of my DEA work happened right at the beginning."

"What do you mean?"

"Without getting into too much detail, I was fresh out of the military, I was a Ranger, and I spoke Spanish. There was a drug war going on down in Colombia. Still is. But they wanted to take advantage of my training and linguistic skills and put me to use where I could help out in a big way. No one would know about it, though, of course."

The agent went on to tell me how the DEA had sent him to Colombia, in an undercover capacity, to learn as much as he could about the drug cartels—their leaders, their infrastructure, their shipment and distribution tactics, how they made decisions. He spent about a year living there, dividing his time between Cali, Medellin, and Bogota, sending back reports on what he'd learned but otherwise laying as low as possible. He said that he was scared constantly, despite the fact that he could melt into an urban environment fairly easily. Then his contact met him one night in the lobby of a hotel.

"This guy tells me I'm done with the cities," the agent continued. "He says, 'We need you to do something else for us.' All I can think is, what do they want now?"

Within days, the former Ranger was inserted into the jungle.

"I felt like a soldier again," the agent told me. "Boots, camouflage, MREs [Meals-Ready-to-Eat], an M16. My orders were to do more covert reconnaissance, but I'd been placed into a new environment, a jungle environment. I was on my own. My mission was more specific—trying to gather intelligence on who was financing, building, and operating the cocaine factories, as well as on where they were located. But you have to understand, here I was, alone, surrounded by drug lords and their henchmen, Marxist rebels, and right-wing paramilitary groups and death squads. I was terrified. Everybody was armed to the teeth and hated everybody else. I saw corpses everywhere. You don't want to know what these guys did to each other. You don't want to know what I saw."

I was surprised that the agent was sharing so much of his story with me, but he was very careful not to give me too many specifics about his early assignment, just a general description of his activities and a vague chronology of events. I asked him what he meant by referring to it as both the high and low point in his career.

"There were nights during my time in the jungle when I couldn't sleep, nights when I didn't think I'd ever make it back. I'll never forget how empty I felt. Like there was absolutely nothing out there. I looked up at the sky and I couldn't even see the stars—just the black between them. That was the lowest of the low. But I *did* do my job, I *did* fight my fear, and I *did* make it out. We even captured some of those people as a result of my work. That was what made it a high point. I was taking out the bad guys in my own small way, and I was trying to make the world a safer and better place. I was doing what I had to do, and not many other people would have been able to do it."

There is a fundamental difference between bravery and bravado, and I sensed none of the latter in that special agent.

His actions had to do with commitment, not cockiness, and his courage was simply an expression of the drive to fulfill his charge.

TRUTH TO POWER

Bravery is an essential quality in any warrior. What makes that quality different in a *spiritual* warrior is that it involves a moral aspect. Courage is not an end in itself, but a means to altruism, to justice and peace. Some are born with this capability. Others must cultivate it. Over time, as we become more and more self-confident—but only if we follow the path of openness, introspection, and practice—courage isn't beyond anyone.

The world has been blessed by many figures who have possessed the courage, even audacity, to call truth to power. When confronted by an unjust person, situation, or society, these "warriors," often at great personal risk, have spoken out—and taken action. We see examples of this throughout the history of the United States. Whether it was the abolitionist movement that fought to end slavery, the suffrage movement that achieved the right of women to vote, or the labor and civil rights movements that advocated better economic and political conditions for workers, the poor, and minority groups—these movements, and others, have been driven by gutsy (and frequently religious) leaders.

The Bible contains many examples of such leaders as well. Take a look at the young Moses, for instance, when he confronts an Egyptian taskmaster—a person in authority and power over him—beating an Israelite slave. Moses overwhelms him, stops the abuse, and is forced to flee into the wilderness of Midian in order to evade certain death. Years later, after he has grown as a spiritual leader, Moses squares off with Pharaoh himself, the "God-King," the absolute ruler of Egypt and a man with an entire army behind him. None of that deters Moses from his mission. With the bold charge, "Let my people go," Moses—under divine direction and with a newfound confidence in himself and his truth—ultimately brings about the liberation of his people from bondage and despotism.

Moses may be (arguably) the most famous and dramatic of the ancient prophets, but there are other, lesser-known biblical prophets who exemplify the spiritual warrior and his or her willingness to stand up to injustice—and to confront power with truth.

Natan is one of them, and I find him appealing not just because the two of us share the same Hebrew name. He is one of the earliest of the Israelite prophets whose exclusive role is to serve a king, and because his particular king, David, was a man of complex character and intense passions, Natan's job was probably quite a challenge. While David, in defeating the Philistine giant Goliath, and later in greatly expanding the Israelite empire, demonstrates great skill and determination (more on David in the next chapter), he also acts—and acts out—in questionable, sometimes problematic ways.

The most well known of David's battles with his own inner demons is likely the story of his relationship with Bathsheba. In the book of Second Samuel we learn that Saul, Israel's very first king, has died, and that David now occupies the throne in Jerusalem. The people of Israel are in a state of war with the Ammonites and their Aramean allies, but David remains in the citadel of the holy capital. Toward the end of one particular day, as David roams the roof of his royal palace, he notices a very lovely woman who is bathing. He inquires about her, and discovers that her name is Bathsheba. He also finds out that she is the wife of Uriah the Hittite, one of King David's most trusted and loyal captains. Still, David sends a servant to bring her to his bedchamber. After he has sex with her, the king sends her away from the palace. Soon after this event, Bathsheba sends him a short, troubling missive: "I am with child" (2 Samuel 11:5).

In a sinister ploy, David recalls Uriah from the front and asks him how things are going for his forces. Then the king instructs him to return to his house and his beautiful wife for a respite from the fierce fighting. David goes so far as to offer him a gift of food and wine for the evening of romance and carnality that he anticipates Uriah will have with Bathsheba during their brief reunion. If Bathsheba's husband sleeps with her right away, David is off the hook! What more efficient way to explain her pregnancy?

Uriah declines the king's gift and refuses to go home to his wife. Instead, in an expression of fidelity that contrasts sharply with David's machinations, Uriah joins the king's servants and sleeps on the floor at the door of the royal palace. Puzzled by his strange behavior, David asks him why he won't go home. Uriah informs him that he simply *cannot* while his fellow Israelite troops are sleeping in the open field, battling for their country and their lives. David responds (without letting his captain know his real motivation) by saying that he will permit Uriah to return to his men the next day—but only, he insists, after they drink and feast together that night. The king does succeed in getting Uriah drunk, but still fails to get him back home and into Bathsheba's bed.

The next morning, Uriah prepares to leave for the combat zone. David sees him off and hands him a note to be given personally to his commander, Joab. The message contains an order for Joab to post Uriah in the middle of the "hottest" battle he can find. Joab obeys the king's command, and Uriah, unaware of what David has done, falls during the bloody fight. What David does is beyond heinous: he literally turns the noble Uriah into the messenger of his own death. By orchestrating what amounts to a premeditated murder, the Jewish king shows blatant disregard for one of the Ten Commandments that God issued to his own ancestors as the foundation of their faith. With Uriah dead, David takes Bathsheba as his wife and she soon bears him a son.

David's lust for Bathsheba, and his drive to "win" at all costs, leave him a lost soul and lead him into a wilderness of moral and spiritual darkness. Yet it is a darkness that David is not even aware of. This is the point in the narrative when Natan enters the picture, when the king's personal prophet must either act or turn a blind eye to it all.

Natan chooses to confront the king, but he does so in an indirect, though no less courageous, way. The prophet, standing before one of the most powerful (and unpredictable) monarchs in the region, informs the king that he must share a disturbing episode with him, one that David needs to be made aware of and will want to act on.

Natan offers the following story:

> There were two men in one city: the one rich and the other poor. The rich man had many flocks and herds; the poor man had nothing except one little ewe lamb, which he had acquired and reared. It had grown up together with him and with his children, and it ate of his food, and drank of his own cup, and lay in his bosom, and was like a daughter to him. And a traveler came to the rich man, and instead of taking an animal from his own flocks and herds to prepare a meal for the wayfarer, he took the poor man's lamb and prepared it for the man. (2 Samuel 12:1–4)

The story enrages David, and he calls for the rich man's execution. Who is this individual, he asks, someone who could behave with such cruelty toward a person far less fortunate? That the king is so oblivious as to who the terrible sinner Natan alludes to is clear evidence of David's deep moral confusion. David has no justification whatsoever for his behavior or his ignorance. He is the Israelite king, and he, along with his people, are bound by the same eternal covenant with God that was revealed to his forebears at the foot of Mount Sinai many centuries earlier. One of the most observed, revered, and well-known parts of that covenant is the commandment not to murder.

In response to David's inquiry into the identity of the rich man, Natan answers boldly, directly, and with an audacity of spirit: "*You* are the man" (2 Samuel 12:7).

This kind of confrontation takes heart, soul, and guts—even for a prophet. Yet David doesn't lash out in anger at Natan. If anything, he seems to respect the prophet's admonition. When faced with this bitter truth, David comes to realize his crime and confesses to the prophet that "I have sinned against God" (2 Samuel 12:13). Although Natan is very much the spiritual hero of this narrative, something interesting happens to David, a former and future warrior of great stature and credibility, as well: he evolves.

The baby son of David and Bathsheba dies at birth. But another son, Solomon, follows in the wake of this tragedy. I interpret the birth of Solomon, known for his wisdom and judgment, as a sort of metaphor for David's second chance, his gradual return and reclamation of his mantle as the moral and spiritual leader of his people. The messianic line is traditionally ascribed to the house of David, and there is a message embedded in that tradition. As the preceding series of events illustrates, that house was far from a paragon of maturity and virtue. Yet the lesson seems to be that we don't need to be saints in order to be spiritual leaders and warriors. We just need to be honest about who we are, learn from our mistakes, and then work very, very hard not to repeat them.

THE SUBORDINATION OF SELF

Looking within is a vital part of our program of self-empowerment. As Master Funakoshi writes, "If introspection reveals my self to be just, then I will go [to battle] even against a thousand or ten thousand men." Genuine courage is a consequence of self-knowledge, a virtuous character, and a strong will. The karate master explains this idea further: "Make benevolence your lifelong duty. This surely is an important mission. It is a lifelong effort, truly a long journey. An ordinary man will draw his sword when ridiculed and will fight at the risk of his life, but he should not in any way be called a 'courageous' man. A truly courageous man is not disturbed even when suddenly confronted with an unexpected event or crisis, nor angered upon finding himself in situations not of his own making, and this is because he has a great heart and his aim is high."

NO GUTS, NO GLORY

When made aware of his king's immoral actions, Natan keeps his cool. He doesn't get angry, yet with a bold and just heart he approaches David and shares his parable—a parable that ultimately transforms David's character and life. The prophet's courage derives from the confidence in his soul and the truth of his message, but it also arises because of his goal. Natan is not striving for the petty triumph of his ego (through a mind game with a monarch), but for justice itself, for a return to some semblance of the original harmony that was ruptured by David's heinous behavior. He is a warrior less concerned with winning than with bringing about reconciliation and peace. In this sense, Natan is following a dictate from *Pirke Avot:* "Be as bold as a leopard, light as an eagle, swift as a deer, and strong as a lion, in order to do the will of our God in heaven." It is only if our actions have an underlying moral and spiritual motivation that what we refer to as "courage" should be treated as truly meritorious.

At times, the path of the spiritual warrior requires us to subordinate our own needs, desires, and emotions for the sake of a higher purpose. Serenity in the face of crisis is a tremendous challenge, but it can serve as a gateway to heroism.

The Roman general Pompey conquered the land of Judea in 63 B.C.E. For over a century, Judea and its inhabitants were oppressed by a rogues' gallery of power-crazed puppet rulers, men such as Herod and Pontius Pilate. It was a period of tremendous conflict—between Jews and Romans, rich and poor, city dwellers and farmers and herders from the countryside. There was also terrible strife *within* the Jewish community. Competition and corruption suffused the ranks of the priesthood. Pharisees and Sadducees fought for dominance. Jewish Zealots who advocated open rebellion against Rome battled religious authorities who favored cooperation or negotiation.

An extremist group of Jewish fighters, the Sicarii ("daggermen"), entered Jerusalem in the fall of 66 C.E. Along with attacking the Roman troops stationed there, these Jews also assassinated Jewish priests, aristocrats, politicians, and anyone else they viewed as being a Roman sympathizer. The revolutionary sparks

THE CHALLENGE OF THE SOUL

that were ignited—and the seething emotions that were un-leashed—soon grew into a national firestorm. For the next four years, until the brutal and bloody siege of Jerusalem and the final destruction of the Second Temple in 70 C.E., the Great Jewish Revolt convulsed the land.

Yet even after the rebellion was mercilessly suppressed and Jerusalem and Judea lay in ruins, one last Jewish stronghold held on, despite all odds, for a few more years: Masada. Origi-nally built to serve as one of Herod's palace-fortresses, Masada, perched high on a mountain plateau in the Judean Desert, had been taken over by a community of Jews. While their identity is a matter of academic dispute (many scholars believe they were Zealots or Sicarii, while some think they were members of the Essene sect), the community stood fast against numerous failed attempts to breach its walls by Roman soldiers, who had set up legionary camps around the mesa-like fortification.

Following two years of futile efforts, the Roman officers de-vised an alternative plan to conquer Masada. By the spring of 73 C.E., they had built a rampart that led directly to the main gate of the fortress, and after two or three months of siege tactics, Rome's troops finally burst into Masada with a battering ram. What they saw shocked them, however. According to Josephus—the Roman historian who chronicled this period—when the soldiers entered the fortress, they discovered that all the buildings but the food storerooms had been set ablaze, and that Masada's 936 inhabit-ants had committed mass suicide rather than face certain defeat, capture, slavery, or execution by their enemy.

There are many reasons why elements of this dramatic epi-sode may be more legend than fact (not the least of which is that suicide is forbidden in traditional Jewish law). But this national-istic legend is nevertheless a powerful one, which is why it is on Masada that modern Israeli soldiers have taken their oaths to the Jewish State upon completion of basic training. Yet *were* these ancient Jews true spiritual warriors? That they showed bravery is beyond doubt. Does that make them moral and heroic? Their collective suicide may have spared them the humiliation of enslavement and denied the Romans a clear victory, but it also meant that they left nothing behind—no lives, no legacy. As an end in itself, can self-sacrifice of this sort be viewed as noble?

There are other models of self-sacrifice that are not as radical, ones rooted in myth more than historicity, metaphor more than reality. Take the death-rebirth idea. We examined in the previous chapter how the mystics interpreted the hidden meaning of the *mikveh* ritual, how immersion in its sacred waters was viewed as a vehicle that can lead to transformation and renewal. Many biblical stories convey the same concept of "death" as a precursor to "new life." Jonah's descent into the belly of the beast is an example we have already discussed. Another instance that illustrates this dynamic is the scene of the prophet Daniel in the lions' den, where prayer functions as the weapon that ultimately releases him from the jaws of death to continue his mission. Long before Jesus, the profound link between death and "resurrection" was a normative Jewish idea.

This chapter is about courage, and the giving over or subordination of self takes a great deal of it. Jonah and Daniel offer us metaphors of this model, but Judaism also expresses it through the utilization of its myths. One of our fascinating, lesser-known myths concerns the two Messiahs, Messiah ben Joseph and Messiah ben David.

While played down by the rabbis with the advent of Christianity, Judaism has a rich set of mythic traditions about the Messiah and the End of Days. Most involve a series of apocalyptic battles that precede God's eventual rule on earth and the destruction of the forces of evil and chaos. According to the myth of the two Messiahs, this era will begin with the appearance of *Mashiach ben Yosef*, or the Messiah from the line of Joseph. Messiah ben ("son of") Joseph is the warrior-Messiah, and he is imagined as the first commander of the army of Israel in the messianic wars. Though he will achieve many triumphs, his ultimate destiny is to die at the hands of the wicked Armilus, another mythic figure, during a great battle in which Israel is defeated by Gog and Magog. His corpse is left unburied in the streets of Jerusalem for forty days, as no one dares to touch it. At the end of this dark period, *Mashiach ben David,* or the Messiah from the house of David, will appear, and his very first act will be to resurrect his tragic forerunner.

Under the charismatic leadership of Messiah ben David, the second Messiah, the apocalyptic wars continue. God joins the battles of Messiah ben David, and victory is ultimately theirs. The final confrontation occurs on two planes: in heaven, where God vanquishes the celestial princes of the nations of the world, thereby weakening the earthly armies under their protection; and on earth, where God intimidates those armies with fearsome omens and portents. Then the small nation and army of Israel, led by Messiah ben David, is able to destroy its enemies despite their vast superiority in numbers.

Why the need for two Messiahs? According to a different but related tradition, the Messiah was prefigured, metaphorically, in Moses. Yet Moses died before he could lead the people of Israel into the Promised Land. As a result, for the parallel to hold, the Messiah, too, would have to die before accomplishing his great task of eternal redemption. Since, however, the Messiah could not be the true redeemer of God if he did not fulfill that task, the only solution was to allow one Messiah to die (like Moses), and then assign the completion of the work of redemption to a second Messiah.

In this ancient myth about larger-than-life spiritual warriors, it is the first Messiah, Messiah ben Joseph, who seems to me the more compelling and pertinent to this chapter. Why? Because he knowingly, selflessly, and boldly accepts his fate. Messiah ben Joseph gives himself up, and over, to a higher purpose. His act of self-sacrifice is not an end in itself, but a *means* to one—and that end is nothing less than the ushering in of God's blissful sovereignty on earth. Messiah ben Joseph subordinates his role to the second Messiah, the one who actually finishes the job and, in a sense, gets all of the glory.

That takes far more than just courage. It takes humility, trust, and an unwavering devotion to his mission. As a model for us, Messiah ben Joseph is as real as it gets.

AN ANATOMY OF COURAGE

Courage can take many different forms. Aristotle, for instance, makes it very clear that by *courage* he means physical courage. His classic example is a soldier facing death in war. But acting bravely in battle is not sufficient to define this virtue—just look at examples of rash people who act out of impulsivity or inappropriate motives. They can act in the same way. For Aristotle, what differentiates courage from rashness is the use of reason combined with a noble goal. Genuinely courageous people recognize a cause as worthwhile and face danger while knowing what they are doing. This separates the soldier who understands both the goal and the situation he is in from someone who acts from a desire to show off, or who fails to truly understand the danger he confronts.

Since Aristotle's time, we have come to accept another type of courage, often called moral courage. Some modern thinkers have pointed out that, in moral courage, the danger is not to a person's physical well-being (though that is possible) but to his or her social standing, acceptance by peers and colleagues, or financial situation. Issues of moral courage arise frequently in our daily lives. A person confronting his or her peer group over a racist joke displays moral courage, just as does a whistle blower facing ostracism from colleagues or an employee confronting sexual harassment with the likelihood of being dismissed. The fear to be overcome in such cases is not one of physical annihilation but primarily social annihilation—a reputation destroyed, or a life of marginal existence in one's community. What motivates such individuals is still the nobility of the goal, but in this case the goal is justice or respect for human dignity.

While there has been much examination over the years— through literature, poetry, war journals, and religious works—

of physical and moral courage, far less has been explored with regard to a third category: psychological courage. The fear to be surmounted in this context is not physical or social, though at times both can be involved. The central fear we must face here is *psychological* annihilation. As we strive to become better and stronger people, we must muster the courage to confront those irrational fears and anxieties that hold us in bondage. These can range from habits and compulsions (such as drinking or promiscuity) to full-blown phobias (such as a fear of heights or open spaces).

In order to face and overcome these fears, we must have a sense of mission, a belief that our goal is noble. Psychological courage isn't about achieving victory in a fight for a just cause, nor is it about defending a moral principle. It is about the development of a mature and stable self, a self that is capable of positive, healthy, and productive relationships to other people and to your own work, interests, and passions.

Any sort of courage that falls within these diverse categories involves at least two components. First, there must be an internal experience of fear. Second, there must be an external perception of danger or risk. When a situation arises that brings both of these components together, and when we are still able to act with resolve and force despite their presence to accomplish worthy, even sacred objectives, we are acting like warriors.

In the popular imagination, courage is more frequently connected to overcoming fear than danger. That may be because the dangerousness of a situation is very often out of a person's control, while many of us think that fear is a reflection of our personality and character and thus something that we can surmount. And yet, truth be told, fear is not always a phenomenon that is under our control—as science and psychology have helped us come to understand. Maybe that is why when people act against a perceived danger in spite of their fear, they are still considered courageous, even if the danger turns out to be based on a false or exaggerated perception. The concept of courage, when examined deeply, is much more complicated than it appears at first blush.

Self-confidence and common sense also play key roles in this complex dynamic. To skydive without appropriate training would not only be risky, but foolish, and the person who did it would be demonstrating bravado, not bravery. Yet the same activity carried out by someone who is properly trained can be seen as somewhat courageous, at least for the first few times. After more jumps—and the development of more skill and experience—whatever fear that person might have experienced initially would disappear.

It should be clear by now that courage, while an essential step on the path to becoming a warrior, has many manifestations, and that most of them are not relegated to the battlefield. Abolitionists and prophets, advocates and visionaries, soldiers and skydivers—all of these men and women represent different and unique expressions of this important, complicated quality. For some, making a serious commitment to a person, vocation, tradition, or faith takes a great deal of courage. For others, persevering through the pain and grief after the death of a loved one, or through their own personal illness, is an act of bravery. For still others, just holding on to hope in this dark and often frightening period in history is itself a show of boldness that not all of us are capable of.

FORTITUDE AND FAITH

The struggle for personal growth and self-transcendence is a difficult one, but hope can be a powerful weapon as we strive to endure and ultimately surmount life's challenges. There is a link between hope and faith, but the only way to bridge the two is with a leap. We must make a journey into the divine mystery, placing our hope not in a person, system, or state of being, but rather in God, the great Other. Only then does hope transform into faith: a reliance on, and trust in, a higher power. That is when faith can become, paradoxically, both an expression and a *source* of true courage.

Two years after ordination, in the summer of 1996, I traveled through the Caucasus region of southern Russia. While my purpose was similar to the one I'd set for myself three years earlier in Central Asia (to teach, pastor, and bring medicine to those in need), the context was very different. The provinces I visited on my journey—Kabardino-Balkaria, Ingushetia, and North Ossetia—either bordered or were in very close proximity to Chechnya, with whom Russia had been engaged in a vicious war after the largely Muslim territory tried to secede and become an independent state in 1994.

As I explored the area and met with its people, the entire northern Caucasus felt like a combat zone. There were military checkpoints along all of the main roads, particularly at border crossings, where young soldiers holding AK-47s would examine my documents. You could sense the tensions between the various ethnic and religious groups, and at times even see their angry eruptions: burned-out municipal buildings, looted churches, the remains of a local mosque that had been bombed. Because of the conflict in Chechnya, age-old tribal animosities were spilling over everywhere. Due to a conditional ceasefire, there was a lull in the fighting during the summer I was there. The bitter conflict resumed in 1999, and Chechen insurgents stalk the forests to this day.

In contrast to the vast open steppes of Central Asia, the Caucasus was a region of rugged snow-capped mountains and dense wilderness, with wild glacier-fed rivers and streams. It was stunningly beautiful. My host, driver, and guide was a modest and kindly Jewish man in his sixties named Dmitri, and it was his small apartment in Vladikavkaz, the capital of North Ossetia (a Christian enclave surrounded by Muslim provinces), that functioned as my base during my stay—an apartment I shared with his wife, son, and daughter-in-law. Though Dmitri had been born and raised in Chechnya's capital, Grozny, he chose to leave everything behind as he witnessed Chechen nationalism intensify and anti-Semitism increase. He understood early on that war with Russia was imminent. At great personal risk (especially as a Jew), Dmitri took his family and traveled across mountain trails to North Ossetia, where he hoped they'd be able to find a better life.

Dmitri's son spoke decent but broken English, and he served as our go-between. When I asked his father what his harrowing journey to the Ossetian border was like, Dmitri answered in general terms through his son: "Not much eat. Chechens and guns. Bad for Jew, bad for all. New trouble, new start. Is life. Nothing else to do. You go."

I did my work, distributing medicine and meeting with people who had personal situations they needed to discuss with a rabbi (there hadn't been a rabbi in the area for as long as anyone could remember). I also gave a few "underground" talks to Dmitri's Jewish friends and neighbors about Judaism—even away from Chechnya, anti-Semitism was a severe problem in the Caucasus, yet the Jews who had lived in this mountainous part of the world for centuries were still desperate to learn more about their heritage.

Toward the end of my stay, just before I had to fly to Moscow and then back to New York, Dmitri arranged a farewell dinner in my honor. The apartment was packed. All of us made long, heartfelt toasts to each other. By dessert, the table was laden with fresh fruit, but it felt as if vodka had been the main course throughout the entire meal.

After all the guests had departed and most of his family had gone to sleep, I stayed up a bit longer with Dmitri and his son. The toasts and shots of vodka continued. This short, humble man more than twice my age drank me under the table. Though I was at the point where basic conversation was becoming ever more difficult, I was able to muster one last question for the household's patriarch. I asked him what he had learned from his experience of escaping from Chechnya and trying to begin all over again.

Since he was probably at least a little drunk himself, Dmitri opened up to me more than he had in our previous days together: "Pain and fear teach me. Many bad things happen people—we no control. But no hope, no can be life. If I no leave

home, I no live. My family, they no live. I not religious, but I
believe God. I no can do this alone. I believe God. In forest, on
mountain, here. I no alone. I more strong when I no alone."

It is frequently only after we pass through life's darker trials
firsthand that we truly gain a more insightful perspective on our
own suffering, and start to develop empathy for the suffering of
those around us—and then act on it. For many people, it is only
when faith serves as our anchor that we are able to summon the
inner strength and courage we need to work our way through
the existential wilderness.

We are not alone, ever. Yet, sometimes, it takes discomfort to
disclose that truth.

For the German philosopher Friedrich Nietzsche, the most
evolved element in the human personality is the "will to power."
This is the quality that permits the superior individual to rise
above all others and break free of the herd mentality. In this
chapter, I have chosen to highlight people and figures of myth
and fantasy—though spiritual warriors all—because they provide models not of the will to power, but of the will, and the
courage, to *persist*. If they share anything with Nietzsche's Übermensch, or ideal human being, it is a deep knowledge about the
necessity, and spirituality, of the affirmation of life, an elemental
grasp that without fortitude and determination, no fear, trial, or
challenge will ever be surmounted. Our brave perseverance
can carry us through the most terrific of obstacles. While we
need some measure of self-confidence before we take on whatever mission comes our way, and though our initial inclination
might be to achieve our aim by ourselves, we will often need
others to help us. It is our capacity for trust, more than the wish
to rely on ourselves, that will save us when we are tempted to
simply give up.

That is the very heart of faith—the act of courage that intimidates so many of us. When we make the leap of faith, when
we jump feet first into the ungraspable mystery of divinity, there

are no guarantees. Will we reach the other side? Will we be injured in the process? Will we find ourselves in a helpless free-fall, staring headlong into an abyss? These questions serve as our test as seekers. Will we be the type of person who stands, paralyzed by terror and dread, at the very edge of uncertainty, or will we boldly venture forth into terra incognita, into a brave new world of infinite potential and possibility?

5

REACT, ADAPT, SURMOUNT

WE HAVE SEEN in the previous chapter several examples of the importance—even necessity—of courage and perseverance, of how these qualities can empower a single individual to have great impact in the face of overwhelming odds and obstacles. For the spiritual warrior, though, these qualities aren't always going to be enough when we try to overcome life's obstacles. At times, despite all of our bravery, fortitude, commitment, skill, and training, situations will arise that will compel us to step "outside of the box," to respond to certain challenges in new, unconventional, and often improvised ways. It is, paradoxically, *because* we have (hopefully) developed a strong foundation in the fundamentals that we can adapt to new contexts and utilize creative tactics.

When the Great Jewish Revolt was crushed and the Second Temple was destroyed, a diaspora ensued. But Jews remained minorities. Sometimes they were treated well. Other times they were oppressed or killed. Over time, though, they persevered, even thrived. Many Jews who were driven from the land of Israel into exile in Babylonia prospered in the commercial and cultural sectors of that urban, cosmopolitan society. The small Jewish community established flourishing, world-renowned academies in Sura and Pumpeditha, from which the famous Babylonian Talmud evolved, a codex of sacred texts and dialogues on law and life that scholars continue to study to this day.

Although relatively few in number, the Jews of Muslim Spain generated their own golden age, during which, over a period of not much more than a couple of centuries (until the violent conquest of that land by King Ferdinand and Queen Isabella in 1492), some of the greatest Jewish thinkers, mystics, poets, and statesmen emerged and influenced the larger medieval world around them for generations. Thomas Aquinas, the famous Catholic philosopher, thought so highly of Maimonides, the great rabbi and philosopher, for instance, that he respectfully referred to him in his theological works simply as "the Rabbi."

Size doesn't always matter. What matters is commitment and creativity.

THE MOTHER OF ALL UNDERDOGS

Some of history's most successful spiritual warriors have over-come their obstacles and adversaries not by troops or swords, but by fidelity and innovation. As far back as the Bible, the young and diminutive David, long before he became a powerful king, faced the Philistine giant Goliath in a way that illustrates this principle.

In the book of First Samuel, the Israelites are in a state of constant conflict with the Philistines, who control the Mediter-ranean coastline and its many trade routes. The book describes battle after battle as the two peoples struggle for supremacy over the land and its borders. Power and control are in a perpetual state of flux. Yet there is one battle in particular that seems to turn the tide in favor of the Israelites. There is a confrontation near the Valley of Elah, with the Philistine army encamped on one side and the Israelite fighters, led by Saul, on the other. Tension is high. The Philistines send forth their champion, Goliath, to intimidate and taunt their adversaries into submission.

The gigantic Goliath, arrayed in his chain mail and brass helmet, and holding a spear, the shaft of which "was like a weaver's beam," walks onto the open battlefield, stands his ground, and shouts at the Israelites: "Choose you a man, and let him come down to me. If he is able to fight with me, and kill me, then we will be your servants. But if I prevail against him, and kill him, then you shall be our servants, and serve us. I taunt the armies of Israel this day; give me a man, that we may fight together" (1 Samuel 17:8–10).

When Saul and the Israelite soldiers witness this hulking giant before them and listen to his brash, belligerent words, they are gripped by fear. For forty days, Goliath presents himself before the Israelite army, offering the same challenge every time—and each time, the Israelites fail to find and send forth a challenger in response.

David, whose three older brothers are at the front, hears of this humiliation to his people. Though young and inexperienced, he approaches the war zone and says to Saul: "Let no man's heart fail him; I will go and fight with this Philistine" (1 Samuel 17:32). Saul tries to dissuade him, arguing that his youthfulness and lack of professional training will lead him to certain death. But David is persistent and eventually convinces Saul that his belief in both God and himself will allow him to win the day over Goliath. He has no use for body armor, a helmet, or even a sword. David simply takes a staff, five smooth stones, and his sling. Then he crosses the valley and confronts the Philistine.

When Goliath sees this young man, the Israelite who has finally come to do battle with him, he is outraged and filled with contempt. He asks David: "Am I a dog, that you approach me with a staff? Come near to me, and I will give your flesh to the birds of the sky, and to the beasts of the field!" (1 Samuel 17:43–44). David responds with a mixture of spiritual trust and self-confidence: "You come at me with a sword, and with a spear, and with a javelin—but I come to you in the name of the Lord of hosts, the God of the armies of Israel, whom you have taunted. This day the Lord will deliver you into my hand, and I will smite you, and I will take your head from you" (1 Samuel 17:45–46).

Whether David's own defiant words are a reflection of masculine posturing or of intentional misdirection, Goliath is clearly surprised and confused by the situation. David takes advantage of that important fact. He knows full well that he could never overcome Goliath if he fought him head-on and in a conventional fashion with swords and spears. He is no match for the Philistine's size, strength, training, and experience. What the context calls for, and what David utilizes, are creativity, adaptation, and innovation.

Goliath makes the first move, a bull rush toward the diminutive David. The nimble Israelite youth charges toward his enemy as well. As the two near one another, David reaches for one of his stones, places it in his sling, and then hurls the projectile forward with a dexterity that collapses their distance: "And the stone sank into [Goliath's] forehead, and he fell upon the earth. So David prevailed over the Philistine with a sling and a stone, and smote the Philistine, and slew him; but David's hand held no sword. And David ran, and stood over the Philistine, and took his sword, and drew it out of its sheath, and slew him, and cut off his head with it" (1 Samuel 17:49–51). After the death of the Philistines' champion, they flee, pursued by the newly inspired Israelites.

David, the future leader of the Israelites, emerges unbowed and victorious because he uses faith, flexibility, focus, and fierce persistence. The sling and stone that crack the giant's skull are merely extensions of David's will and imagination.

David, despite his enormous character flaws (as we saw in the last chapter), is a model for how a spiritual warrior might act when confronted by a seemingly insurmountable challenge. This image of the biblical David does not mirror the restrained and serene version that was sculpted by Michelangelo many centuries later and that stands, still and almost complacent, in

Florence. The true David is better characterized by a fiery pugnacity, by guts, and by an absolute refusal to submit to conventional tactics. He is a metaphor for anyone seeking the warrior's path—a path of openness, determination, and courage. These are the qualities that make creativity possible.

THE INNOVATION OF IMPROVISATION

Whether in the military arts or the fine arts, the role of improvisation is crucial. The same applies to the art of spiritual growth. As situations and contexts change, we must respond to those changes and evolve with them—without ever compromising our basic principles. When we say that someone is "quick on their feet," what we mean is that they possess the skill to adapt to new and unanticipated events. Since no one can predict with certitude what will occur within the next year, let alone within the next five minutes, we must accept the fact that life is, fundamentally, a mystery. Our ability to respond effectively to that mystery, rather than becoming paralyzed by it, helps to define us.

What constitutes a "successful" soul? Probably some very similar traits that help make paintings and battles successes or failures (in addition to the healthy integration of NaRaN that I discussed in the introduction). Look at the example of Jackson Pollock, a master of abstract expressionism. Though he went to art school for a time and had a reasonably strong grounding in the fundamentals of his craft, it wasn't until he accidentally dripped paint onto a canvas that he truly discovered his particular self-expression as a painter. What for many artists might have been a problem—splotches of paint mingling with other colors or interfering with a well-planned sequence of shapes, forms, or figures—Pollock viewed as an unexpected opportunity to improvise, and he used the "accident" to his advantage, creating dozens of striking, dynamic, provocative, and extremely powerful works of art that now hang in museums around the world.

The improvisation *became* the innovation, and it made Pollock a world-famous individual and a success as an artist and painter. As his confidence in his improvisational skills grew, he went so far as to let cigarette butts, chewing gum wrappers, and other foreign objects that fell onto his works-in-progress simply remain where they landed; Pollock just painted around or over them, incorporating them into the finished product. With this no-holds-barred attitude and approach, he was able to transform the mundane, disposable "stuff" of our everyday lives into something transcendent. Today, Pollock's drip works are considered masterpieces of the bold new genre that he helped invent.

As I have tried to illustrate through the examples of the very modern Jackson Pollack, and the very ancient David, what I mean by achieving success is related not merely to utilizing unorthodox techniques or tactics, but to being prepared in advance to respond to the unexpected and unforeseen. It is only if we stand in a vigilant state of readiness for the unanticipated that we will be able to adapt and innovate when challenges come our way. Context leads to creativity, and creativity leads to innovation. Whatever the scale of our challenge, if we are up to the task, it is at this point that our training, will, and heart will serve as the engines that put our reactions into practice.

Another example of how receptivity and creativity can lead to success is the story of Hanukkah. The holiday is known to and observed by Jews around the world, but the details of this commemoration of the Jewish military triumph over King Antiochus and his Syrian-Greek occupiers are not very familiar to most people. Over two millennia ago, Antiochus and his army conquered the Holy Land, plundered and burned Jerusalem, and desecrated the Temple with idols. Jews were murdered, abused, and forbidden to practice their faith. The troops of Antiochus were well armed, well trained, and sizeable in number. But the Jews had something on their side that the Syrian-Greeks lacked—a history of experience with foreign occupation and oppression. From the Egyptians to the Babylonians to the Persians, the Jewish people had felt the heavy yoke of alien domination for many centuries, and they were braced for this new onslaught.

The story begins in the small village of Modi'in, which had become a hotspot of Jewish agitation. Incensed by the unexpected and unacceptable situation, an elderly priest named Mattathias makes the first move toward open rebellion against the occupation. When the foreign soldiers enter Modi'in in a show of force, and a fellow Jew offers a sacrifice on a pagan altar, Mattathias kills the man as well as one of the king's officers. Then the priest, his five sons, and their followers flee to the Judean hills, leaving all of their possessions behind.

As news of this incident spreads across the land in the weeks and months that follow, other Jews join the new rebel leader, Judah Maccabee, son of Mattathias, who died soon after their escape from Modi'in, and abandon their homes for the relative safety of the forests, hills, and mountains. King Antiochus starts to assemble his troops to put down the insurrection. At this point, all he has in his favor is the size and strength of his force. There is no element of surprise, no momentum, no popular support. Growing numbers of Jewish fighters have already placed themselves in hiding, waiting in caves.

As the first major military confrontation nears, some fellow Jews express their trepidation to Judah. He replies by saying that "victory in war does not depend upon the size of the [adversary's] force; the strength comes from heaven" (1 Maccabees 3:19).

Using spontaneity, adaptation, and improvisation as weapons, Judah and his followers use their natural surroundings to their advantage. Though greatly outnumbered, Judah's ingenuity and guerilla tactics allow him to outmaneuver his enemy. When the Syrian-Greek troops are drawn onto the slopes of the Judean hills, their tight phalanxes fall apart, separating the soldiers from one another and leaving them highly exposed; their chariots get stuck in the mud and become useless. Inspired Jewish fighters then attack the armor-laden enemy swiftly and efficiently, emerging by surprise from caves and woods and leaving their opponents bewildered and afraid. In battle after battle, Judah and his fighters triumph over the much larger force, retake their land, and reconsecrate the Temple in Jerusalem.

These key principles for success—adaptation, improvisation, innovation—are as applicable to the world of spirituality and religion as they are to the fields of art and war. As I noted at the outset of this chapter, the golden age for the Jews of Spain came to an unexpected and abrupt end in 1492 when they were expelled from what had been their home for centuries. Jews all over the region were in a state of shock and trauma. The effects of the expulsion should not be underestimated; one of the primary (and most creative) branches of the Jewish people was forcibly uprooted, and one of its most powerful spiritual movements, Kabbalah, was ruptured. The Jewish people needed to regain its psychic footing, and Jewish mysticism had to find new teachers and paths.

In the period that followed, classical Kabbalah, just as the Jewish community as a whole, had to adapt to new conditions and challenges. Its teachers, while steeped in the traditional texts and practices, knew that if mysticism was to survive it would have to evolve. A small band of young rabbis who lived in the Galilean hilltop town of Safed used this as an opportunity to create fresh practices and innovative ideas. Rather than allowing Kabbalah to ossify or perish, they reconstructed it in their own, unique image.

Probably the best known and most influential member of this group was their leader, Rabbi Isaac Luria (who died in 1572 at the age of only thirty-eight). Under Luria's guidance, his circle of disciples turned the sixteenth century into yet another "golden age"—at least as far as Jewish mysticism is concerned—and developed what is now referred to as Lurianic Kabbalah, a bold mystical system of metaphysical beliefs, theosophical mythologies, and esoteric spiritual practices. One of its most unconventional, even irreverent ideas is that of *tzimtzum,* an idea through which Luria and his followers completely overturned (and in some important ways rejected) mainstream Jewish beliefs about the creation of the world and God's relationship to it.

The concept of tzimtzum, or contraction, posits a starkly different explanation of the world's beginning than does the first chapter of the book of Genesis. According to Lurianic Kabbalah, all of existence was initially suffused with the divine presence—leaving space for absolutely nothing else. In order for the heavens, the earth, oceans, forests, mountains, and all living things to come into being, God had to take a step back, or withdraw, so as to make room for them. God's first act was not to create, as the verses of the Torah tell us, but to *recoil*. Only then was creation itself even a possibility.

Whatever you think about Luria's ideas, his capacity and willingness to think in new ways, his intellectual dexterity and spiritual creativity, his fearlessness to take on the religious status quo, his ability to transform a challenge into an opportunity—all these help to make him a prime example of the spiritual warrior we have been exploring in this book. What he succeeded in fighting against was the death of a movement. What he fought for was its evolution, and in doing so his influence lives on.

THE SCALPEL AND THE PEN

We have discussed a number of historical examples from art, warfare, and religion to try to illuminate some basic concepts and principles for achieving success and empowerment. We have also seen that how we respond to the unforeseen and unexpected can offer insights into who we are and who we might yet become, how obstacles and perceived barriers can become opportunities for change and growth if we act in ways that are sometimes unconventional and improvised. Life, like death, is a fundamental mystery: Anything can happen to anybody at any time. Will we be ready?

I had a brush with death—or, more accurately, I had what I *perceived* to be a brush with death—at the age of three. During a routine examination, my pediatrician discovered an irregularity with my heart. After a series of tests (which I imagine must have been completely heart-wrenching for my mother and father) I was diagnosed with PDA, patent ductus arteriosus. What this meant, I'd later learn from my own physician father, was that a shunt that connected two of the most important arteries next to my heart had not properly closed upon birth. Blood was unnecessarily, and dangerously, flowing through it, causing undo strain on my young cardiovascular system. A surgeon would need to open me up, tie off the shunt, and then sew me back together. To this day, whenever I look in the mirror, I see the scar from that operation: a light purple line that coils around my left side, like a snake, from my pectoral muscle all the way up to my shoulder blade.

After forty years, I can still recall images and feelings from that early childhood experience—an experience that, as a three-year-old, I could not fully comprehend. All I sensed was that there was something wrong with me, that people—especially my parents—were extremely concerned about me, and that I was confused and scared.

One memory that remains vivid is how I reacted whenever a doctor walked into my hospital room. Despite reassurances from my mother or a nurse, I would become filled with fear, climb out of my bed, and run to hide behind a different bed somewhere in the room. Another image relates to the removal of my stitches. I can see the doctor, unfamiliar tools in hand, manipulating the silk threads that had held my severed skin together for weeks. I can even remember the cold metal table that I had to sit on, silently, not sure if I should trust this strange man who seemed to be infringing on my body.

My parents arranged a surprise party for me when I returned home. But I didn't understand. Who were all of these people? And why were they all so focused on me?

A sense of *invasiveness* surrounded this entire episode in my life, and even though I was a young child, I know that it caused me long-lasting distress and discomfort. I was a very shy child for a very long time, but as I grew older and started school, I began to open up to others. Yet it was to myself that I opened up the most, and in a particular way—through the written word. As I look back at my youth, it seems pretty clear to me that creative writing was linked in a powerful way to my operation;

literary expression, and the act of creation itself, somehow helped me to cope with whatever psychological pain I must have experienced. My response to that pain was to write: poems, journal entries, short stories. I wrote in school, during summer camp, at home.

Human mortality was always a theme and a thread that was interwoven with whatever I wrote. My awareness of content, however, came later. At the time, what I loved most was the journey, the struggle to find just the right word in a sentence or verse, to see the arrangement of paragraphs on a page, to listen to the music that it all made. Yet I was interested in more than creating beautiful things. I needed a path—and one that felt safe—through which I could express myself, a path through which I could respond to life's mysteries and convey my own feelings and thoughts of wonderment and terror.

As I matured, I think that my self-consciousness about my congenital heart defect gradually spilled over into a larger sense of "defect," or marginality, about myself in relation to the world around me. Today, I can read through my books, sermons, and lectures and discern an obvious pattern of preoccupation with matters of life and death, with the challenge of the human condition itself. Through my writing, I am able to temporarily distance myself from reality so as to better understand, confront, and ultimately, reintegrate with it. The book you are holding in your hands is a manifestation of that impulse and drive to sever myself from the world in order to better relate to it.

I suspect that my passion to push boundaries, often in a physical way, is connected (perhaps unconsciously) to that same childhood operation and my perceived brush with mortality. Why else have I actively searched out activities and environments that have inevitably tested me—whether sea kayaking in the frigid Arctic Ocean, chasing twisters through Tornado Alley, or practicing karate forms in the Amazon—if some deep hunger wasn't being fed in the process, a craving to face, and transcend, my finitude?

A primary lesson of the personal and historical stories in this book is that, if we are open, bold, and creative, we can transform challenges into opportunities, seemingly insurmountable battles into great victories. We can *evolve*—though that evolution will almost always involve struggle. Freud thought that struggle was at the heart of human nature. He argued that the conflict took place between our instinct for life and our instinct for death, between the id, ego, and superego, between the conscious and the unconscious. For Erik Erikson, one of Freud's disciples, our conflicts do not occur in a vacuum but rather with other people and the outside world. In Erikson's psychoanalytic model, each of the eight stages of human development is marked by a crisis, or turning point. We can either master the developmental challenge or fail to resolve the core struggle.

If we deal successfully with life's existential conflicts (such as identity versus role confusion, or intimacy versus isolation), we evolve as human beings; if we fail to work through them, we stagnate. There is continuity in human development, and this continuity is reflected in the stages of growth: each stage is related to and affected by the others. In the previous chapter, we saw how a DEA agent's dark night of the soul led to a sense of professional and personal fulfillment and a fresh, revivified approach to living. We also saw how, even in the throes of great hardship and struggle, my friend Dmitri was able to summon the hope and faith that helped lead him and his family to a new life in a new land.

MEANS AND ENDS

The ways in which we can use creative, unconventional tactics to succeed in achieving our goals are easy to see in the martial context. The United States military, for instance, has developed elite units (such as the Special Forces and Navy SEALS) devoted specifically to this task. What these kinds of units share is a "whatever works" philosophy of combat, based on adaptation, improvisation, and innovation. It is the situation, and the actions of the enemy, that dictate strategy. Fighters in these small units are trained to change their plans on the spot when necessary, to use surprise as a weapon, to take advantage of their natural surroundings, to move quickly and unpredictably, to conduct psychological warfare, and to harness the latest technology (unmanned drones for surveillance and attacks, laser-guided missiles, cyber-strikes) in their operations.

Many of these tactics trace back to antiquity. We have already discussed how David and the Maccabees triumphed over their larger and stronger opponents by using ingenuity as their greatest weapon, but there are other examples. When Joshua leads the Israelites into the Promised Land, he must first conquer the fortified city of Jericho before they can advance any further. The Bible makes it clear that psychological warfare plays an essential role in this battle: Joshua has seven priests march around Jericho's walls seven times, blowing their ram's horns as they move, before he sends in troops against the cowed city. Genghis Khan and the Mongols, who conquered vast swaths of territory, were masters of speed, mobility, and adaptation to ever-changing environments (as I witnessed firsthand when I traveled and camped with modern-day Mongolian nomads a few years ago). And Maori warriors, before engaging an enemy tribe, would first try to intimidate and terrify them with their fierce-looking tattoos, war dances, and chants.

Yet innovative, even brilliant tactics in and of themselves are value neutral; what matters for our purpose is the particular objective for which they are utilized—that is, the morality of the mission. Frequently, in war as in spirituality, the question of morality, of whether the "end justifies the means," can be a very difficult one to answer.

For spiritual warriors, the role of creativity is just as important to their work, but it is often more subtle and harder to detect. Esther is a case in point. The biblical book of Esther, read during the joyous holiday of Purim, is the audacious tale of one woman's bold and determined effort to fight against her fate and that of her people, the Jews.

The book (more often referred to as a megillah, or scroll) of Esther opens with a lavish banquet that is being held by Ahasuerus, the king of Persia, in his royal palace in the imperial capital of Shushan. The feast is meant to honor Ahasuerus himself, who, by his third year as king, "reigned from India to as far as Ethiopia, and ruled over one hundred and twenty-seven provinces" (Esther 1:1). On the seventh day of this months-long celebration, the king, whose heart is "merry with wine," orders his queen, Vashti, to appear before the assembled princes, noblemen, officers, and courtiers so that he can show off her beauty. But Vashti refuses. Enraged at this public rebuke, Ahasuerus banishes her from the palace forever. As a result of this action, the king must now find a new queen, so he sends his servants to scour the lands of his vast empire to seek out, and bring to Shushan, lovely young virgins from whom he will choose another wife. One of those women is Esther, a young Jew whose true Hebrew name is Hadassah. An orphan, Esther has been raised and cared for by a relative, Mordecai, right in the capital city.

All of the young virgins are eventually presented to Ahasuerus, and the beautiful Esther catches the king's eye: "The girl pleased him, and she received kindness from him. He speedily gave her ointments, and her portions, and the seven maidens chosen to be given to her from the king's house. And he moved her and her maidens into the best place of the house of the women" (Esther 2:9). Ensconced in the king's harem, Esther does not reveal her secret identity as a Jew, for the potential elevation of a Jew to the status of royalty would have been unthinkable in Persia, and Mordecai had already cautioned her to hide her religious identity. Over a period of several months, Ahasuerus "tries out" the choicest virgins, but in the end, it is Esther he most desires: "The king loved Esther above all other women, and she won more grace and favor with him than all the virgins, so that he set the royal crown upon her head and made her queen instead of Vashti" (Esther 2:17).

Time passes, and after Esther discovers and discloses a plot to assassinate the king (thanks to Mordecai, who overhears the plan and conveys the information to her), Ahasuerus's love for his queen grows into a deep trust in her as well. Subsequent to these events, Haman, a sinister anti-Semite, is promoted to a seat above all of the other nobles. Everyone in the kingdom bows down to him—except Mordecai, whom he passes near the palace gate. This inflames Haman's anti-Semitism, and he decides not only to have Mordecai killed, but to exterminate *all* of the Jewish people within the kingdom.

As part of his own plot, Haman gives disinformation to the king in order to manipulate his emotions: "There is a certain people scattered abroad and dispersed among the people in all the provinces of your kingdom; their laws are different from every other people, and they do not keep the king's law. It is not in the king's interest to tolerate them. If it please the king, let it be written that they may be destroyed" (Esther 3:8–9). Ahasuerus gives Haman permission to move forward with his plans for ethnic cleansing, and Haman wastes no time. He dispatches couriers to all of the provinces in the empire, each bearing letters containing a royal decree to exterminate every Jewish man, woman, and child. The king has no idea his own wife belongs to this people.

Mordecai becomes aware of Haman's actions and murderous intentions and transmits this information to Esther. Faced with this horrific situation, how should she respond? Like David and the Maccabees, Esther thinks outside of the box and improvises—this is a time for creative, unconventional, even uncomfortable tactics.

The story makes it clear that Esther is scared. She knows that it is against Persian law for anyone, even the queen, to enter the king's innermost court without an official invitation. The standard punishment for violating this law is execution. Yet Esther summons the strength and the courage to surmount her fear and decides to risk death in order to address Ahasuerus in private and to try to save her people. She could take the easy way out by ignoring their plight, enjoying her royal comforts and protection, and continuing to hide her true identity as a Jew.

Instead, Esther sends word to Mordecai: "Go, and gather together all the Jews who are in Shushan, and fast for me. Do not eat or drink for three days, night or day. I and my maidens will also fast. Then I will go in to the king, though it is against the law. And if I perish, I perish" (Esther 4:16).

While Mordecai has been Esther's source of information, it is she alone who must act, and in a way that might very well lead to her own self-sacrifice. On the third day, Esther dons her royal apparel and stands silently in the inner court of the king's private house, facing the throne. The sight of Esther standing vulnerably in his inner court, dressed in all her finery, moves the king, and rather than having her sentenced to death, Ahasuerus extends his golden scepter (so that Esther may "touch the tip") and then invites her inside. After all, he loves and trusts her. The king asks Esther what it is that she so desires: "Even if it is half the kingdom, it will be given to you" (Esther 5:3).

This is the moment where Esther, through the use of both seduction and manipulation (the most effective tools at her disposal), sets her counterplot into motion. She informs Ahasuerus that she wants to hold a banquet for Haman, presumably to honor his "vigilance" as the king's right-hand man and for having revealed disloyal subjects within his empire. Ahasuerus accedes to her reasonable request, and Haman immediately accepts the invitation to have himself feted in the royal palace. Although he is not aware of it yet, Haman has just sealed his own doom. Esther, through her machinations, words, and ingenious strategy, soon proves herself to be a sort of Jewish Trojan horse.

The celebration begins, and on the second day of the "banquet of wine," the (drunken?) king once again asks the wife he loves so dearly if there is anything more she desires. With her husband pliant and her adversary present, Esther is now ready to make her move. She replies: "If I have found favor in your sight, O King, and if it please the king, let my life be given to me at my petition, and my people at my request. For we are sold, I and my people, to be exterminated, to be slain, and to perish" (Esther 7:3–4).

Incensed that anyone would dare to have his beloved Esther

and her people slaughtered, the king demands to know the identity of the person behind the plan. "The adversary and enemy," Esther says, "is this wicked Haman!" (Esther 7:6). Outmaneuvered by a member of the very people he wants to liquidate, Haman is left speechless. He is summarily hanged on the same gallows that had been originally constructed for Mordecai in retaliation for his insubordination. Ahasuerus has the letters of extermination recalled from all the provinces of his kingdom, and the earlier order is rescinded. Esther's victory is now complete. She has eliminated a vicious opponent, rescued the Jewish people from destruction, and finally disclosed her true identity.

Esther, with the help of Mordecai, is the heroine of this story, yet she must utilize deception, sexuality, and manipulation in order to achieve her goals. Do the ends justify the means? Does Esther behave in ways that are heroic and moral, or are her actions simply necessary in light of the troubling context in which she finds herself? The answer, to me, is murky. What is clear is that it is only through her creative (though morally ambiguous) tactics that she is able to save her people and herself from tragedy.

EMBRACE THE UNCOMFORTABLE

What *is* creativity, and how can it help us to grow and mature as spiritual beings? Over the years and centuries, the quality of creativity has been attributed variously to divine intervention, cognitive processes, our social environment, personality traits, and sometimes even chance ("a lucky accident," "serendipity," and the like). It has been associated with genius, mental illness, and humor. Some claim creativity is a trait that we are born with; others argue it can be taught with the application of basic techniques.

Although popularly associated with art and literature, creativity is also an essential part of innovation and invention in a vast array of other fields, such as business, economics, architecture, industrial design, science, and engineering. We have already discussed how important a role it plays in the military arena, as well as in our biblical narratives and religious history. Creativity is what gave birth to Creation itself, whether you believe in the version from Genesis or in the mythic ideas of Lurianic Kabbalah.

Experience teaches us that we must react, adapt, and act creatively (and at times daringly) if we are to surmount our challenges. Erich Fromm, whom I cited in the first chapter, writes: "Creativity requires the courage to let go of certainties." What might he mean by this statement? Certitude offers safety and comfort, even as it constricts and imprisons us. That is the paradoxical attraction of religious fundamentalism, authoritarianism, ideologues, and any other sort of black-or-white thinking, system, or human attitude. It takes an act of courage to let go of our dogmatism, to embrace the uncertainty that makes evolution and outside-the-box thinking and behavior possible.

Courage and creativity must be interwoven in the soul of the spiritual warrior.

Fromm has more to say on the subject: "Conditions for creativity are to be puzzled; to concentrate; to accept conflict and tension; to be born every day; to feel a sense of self." This idea of learning not just to tolerate but to *embrace* life's uncertainties, ambiguities, conflicts, and tensions is an indelible part of a healthy and successful approach to facing our challenges. We can never create if we are too afraid to take risks, including the risk of failure. And we can never really be free to think and act in ways that afford us with the opportunity to mature and develop unless we have a powerful sense of self, a deep feeling that at each and every instant we are born and reborn, in perpetuity.

In the Jewish morning liturgy, we recite the following words: "Praised are You, Adonai our God, Sovereign of the universe, Creator of light and darkness, who makes peace and brings all things into being. In mercy, You illumine the world and those who live on it. In Your goodness You renew, day after day, forever, the works of creation."

The last line of this daily prayer might seem redundant at first, but its focus on perpetual renewal (and on the fact that we should not take such a miraculous gift for granted) makes each word essential. From the time we are born until our moment of death, we all are going through a constant process of birth and rebirth as new beings with new opportunities for personal growth and advancement. This is a profound spiritual lesson. The knowledge that self-transformation is ongoing and always possible, that whatever mistakes we make or problems we might encounter can be improved, corrected, or transcended at some future point, is a much-needed message of empowerment and hope as we engage with our opponents, be they external adversaries or internal demons.

The cliché that urges us to "roll with the punches" is more than an aphorism for combat and confrontation—it is a weapon for survival and growth. We must always be ready to act and evolve in the face of the unanticipated. Changes in society, culture, and world events led to the Reformation in Christianity; changes brought about by the ideas of modernity led to the various movements that emerged from traditional Judaism. Obstacles only become opportunities if we let them. And we let them by being prepared.

In our own work as spiritual seekers, we must remain ever vigilant, and we must strive to cultivate within ourselves a predisposition to anticipate and prepare for the unexpected, to react and adapt to new situations and contexts, to innovate and overcome. This will require self-confidence, as well as commitment, training, openness, and all of the other skills and qualities that we have discussed throughout this book. It will also necessitate a great capacity to *endure*—and it is to that important topic that we now turn.

6

THE STAMINA OF SPIRIT

You might be the best technical martial arts practitioner in the world—your strikes, kicks, throws, submission holds, and kata might look absolutely majestic—but if you can't take a punch, then you are not really a true fighter. You're just an aesthetician. Real fighters know how important it is to simply stand your ground, especially when you're taking a pummeling. Ray Mancini, once a world champion boxer, told me that he never approached a fight with the "big picture" in his head; he treated every single round as a separate and independent bout, every exchange with his opponent and every second on the timer as ends in themselves. He would focus only on the moment at hand.

Fighting was about being fully present and exposed, standing half-naked before a crowd of strangers. Mancini attributes his past wins to endurance, to the stamina that carried him through the challenges of exhaustion, humiliation, and the pain inflicted on him by the person he was fighting. That stamina was the result of training and conditioning, but only up to a certain point.

What mattered the most to him, what helped him to push past his body's physical limits, was how well connected he was to his heart.

That is how fighters become champions—having heart, never backing down, and never giving up. While skill is key, drive and desire earn victories and title belts.

The same dynamic is true in the metaphysical arena, where the path to becoming a spiritual warrior and striving for self-transcendence can be just as demanding on our souls. Without heart, without a passion to persevere against all odds and through any obstacle, we will always fall short of our goals. We must learn to endure our pain and recover from our wounds if we are to progress and grow. How do we bounce back after we've been knocked down—not by a prizefighter in a ring, but by human experience?

LEAPING FOR HEAVEN

Rabbi Abraham Joshua Heschel first pointed out the theological link (and spiritual affinity) between the Kotzker Rebbe and Kierkegaard. I explored the two thinkers myself in my book *God at the Edge*. While we will discuss Kierkegaard at length in the following chapter, let's turn now to the Kotzker, since his life and thought are so powerfully connected to the notion of stamina and its necessity on the human journey.

Rabbi Menachem Mendel of Kotzk was born in 1787 near Lublin, Poland, and from very early on he was a controversial figure within the Hasidic movement. While the founder of this mystical movement, the Ba'al Shem Tov, emphasized joy and love in his spirituality, the Kotzker Rebbe advocated constant combat against egocentricity as the path toward inner development and self-transcendence. His view is in clear alignment with that of the Gaon of Vilna who, as we have noted, saw life as a perpetual tug-of-war between NaRaN, the interrelated but competing levels of our own souls.

While Hasidism's founder preached about the warm and

immanent presence of God in the world, the Kotzker taught that an enormous and permanent chasm separated God from the world. In his radical (and very public) departure from the religious worldview—and emotional attitude—of the Ba'al Shem Tov, the Kotzker Rebbe inevitably became a disquieting figure on the outer fringes of his community, and he had to endure a life and a career of social marginality. Yet the Kotzker wasn't concerned about collecting disciples or connecting with the masses. His ultimate objective was to uncover the Truth, and for the Kotzker, Truth was buried far away from mortal sight.

There is always the possibility of hope, however, in the Kotzker's approach to life. If we have the drive to persist, the will to evolve, and the capacity to face and overcome adversity, we will move forward, even if it takes a divine hand to guide us.

The Kotzker never wrote down his teachings. Fortunately for us, though, his son-in-law wrote about his life, and his followers, though relatively few in number, recorded the sayings, aphorisms, and parables of their master. For me, one parable in particular captures the essence of the Kotzker Rebbe's spiritual vision and his attitude toward human life—and shows the link with this chapter's core concept.

The Kotzker teaches that all souls descend a ladder from heaven down to earth, a different ladder for each soul. Once they have arrived, the ladder is removed. In time, they are ordered to ascend back to heaven. The Kotzker writes:

Some despair and do not even try to ascend because their ladder is gone. Others jump up and fall, again and again, until they, too, give up. But a few souls [those I would consider warriors] refuse to surrender, despite the apparent foolhardiness and futility of leaping and crashing back down to earth. "We must do what God asks of us," they say, "no matter the consequence of our actions or the impossibility of our task." They leap and leap, and plummet over and over to the ground, until—in an act of mercy—God ultimately draws them up to heaven.

For the Kotzker, it is through stamina, through never giving up despite the apparent futility, even absurdity, of our actions, that transcendence comes to human beings. When we "leap" toward God (or confront, struggle, and do battle with those forces that threaten to hold us back from our spiritual growth), we are striving not for the known, but for the *un*known. That is faith. There is no guarantee that we will not be wounded through our efforts. Yet human effort alone is not sufficient for the realization of transcendence. For that we need divine aid. The mystical ladder that linked our primordial souls to God is gone. A gap now divides us from the divine, a void of egocentricity and human constriction. The petty distractions that root us to the material world hinder our vision of the world of the spirit; the reason that produces scientific knowledge cannot fathom a transcendent God, a God who transcends reason itself.

Faith is more than a challenge. It is pain. For God's reality is interconnected with God's absence, the sense of separation we feel so frequently in our everyday lives.

In the end, God is the only answer to our needs and yearnings. But first, in spite of the discomfort it might cause us, we must acknowledge, express, and work hard to satisfy our desires. In a related parable, the Kotzker illustrates this important point. The prophet Elijah chances upon a hunter in the wilderness. He inquires as to why the man is living alone in the wilderness without the divine guidance of the Torah. The hunter responds by saying, "Because I was never able to find the gate that leads to the presence of God."

"You were certainly not born a hunter," Elijah notes. "So from whom did you learn to follow this calling?"

"My need taught me," answers the hunter.

Then the prophet says in response, "And had your need been equally great because you had lost your way very far from God, do you think it would have failed to show you the way to Him?"

Through this parable, the Kotzker seems to be showing us that God's presence has less to do with external reality than with our own inner lives. We must acknowledge the uncomfortable fact that we are lost, express our deep need to connect with the divine, and then make a serious effort to cultivate that relationship. God is waiting for us, but if we don't make a concerted (and possibly lifelong) attempt to find God, if we give up too quickly, we will remain befuddled in a spiritual wasteland. "Where is God?" the Kotzker asks elsewhere. "In any place where He is given entry." He also says, "One who does not see the Omnipresent in every place will not see Him in any place." Whether or not God plays an active role in our lives is ultimately up to us. If we can't find "the gate" to the divine, it is not because we are searching in the wrong places, but because we are not searching hard enough. If the hunter in the story put as much time and intensity into tracking down God as he does into chasing game, he'd find far more than food.

We are all hunters, and we are all lost in a (sometimes hostile) wilderness. Adversity is just part of the human condition. What defines us as warriors, though, is possessing the courage to fully accept that truth—and the stamina to respond to it.

WHO WILL BE FOR ME?

As is the case with many of the experiences, practices, and principles we have explored in this book, there is an element of risk that is always present whenever we venture out into the new and unknown. At times, our journeys and challenges will take place in the company of others; much of the time we must face them alone. Yet individual initiative is often the key to our success and, sometimes, even to our survival. As the Jewish sage Hillel instructs us, "If I am not for myself, who will be for me?"

From his own observations as a concentration camp prisoner in Dachau and Buchenwald, Bruno Bettelheim concluded that the inmates who gave up and perished were the ones who had also given up any effort to act with personal autonomy, who had fallen prey to their captors' goal of dehumanizing and exercising absolute control over them. Bettelheim thought that even the smallest and (on the surface) most insignificant expressions of a dynamic and persistent will—for instance, an inmate deciding whether to eat a piece of bread he or she had been given right at that moment or to store it away for future consumption—could literally mean the difference between life and death.

It was the resolve to keep living—and a hope that their ordeal would come to an end—that served as the most effective weapon in the prisoners' fight to go on.

Although most of us will never have to go through the kind of horrific experience described above, we all face hardships at different points during the course of our own lives. Yet it frequently takes a challenging event or an arduous episode to demonstrate just how resolute our wills actually are, or can become, if really put to the test.

There's a wonderful scene in the classic Tennessee Williams play *The Night of the Iguana,* through which the playwright captures and conveys the powerful, almost salvific role that raw and unrelenting stamina can play on our own spiritual journeys. Shannon is a troubled man at war with himself, a defrocked minister "at the end of his rope." Hannah is a kind and compassionate woman he meets at a secluded hacienda in Mexico. Shannon pleads with her to help him get through his dark night of the soul:

> Hannah: I can help you because I've been through what you are going through now. I had something like your spook—I just had a different name for him. I called him the blue devil, and . . . oh . . . we had quite a battle, quite a contest between us.
>
> Shannon: Which you obviously won.
>
> Hannah: I couldn't afford to lose.
>
> Shannon: How'd you beat your blue devil?
>
> Hannah: I showed him that I could endure him and I made him respect my endurance.

Whether we call them spooks, blue devils, inner demons, or simply obstacles, all of us will encounter moments of challenge, or (con)tests, in our lives. If we try to deny that reality, all we will do is stunt our own inner growth. Like existential prizefighters, we must have confidence in ourselves, and we must tap in to our capacities for resilience and fortitude—even in the face of struggle and suffering. While, ultimately, we must endure our "blue devils" alone, we can learn—and gain inspiration from—the behavior of others. How do we develop character? How do we transcend adversity? For Aristotle, the answer is clear: follow the example of someone who is *already* in the place we want to be.

With that in mind, let's return to the example of Resh Lakish, one of the ancient spiritual warriors whom I discussed earlier in the book. According to a passage in the Talmud, "One who witnessed Resh Lakish engaged in debate would think he was uprooting mountains [from the earth] and grinding them against each other."

What is this passage trying to teach us? Resh Lakish was a powerful man, both physically and spiritually. He had training and experience as a gladiator before turning his focus and energy to matters of the spirit and transforming himself into a great rabbinic sage. Yet in whatever he did, he possessed fortitude and passion—he had heart—and that fact played an essential role in his success in everything he was faced with. The Hebrew word for "heart" is *lev,* and it is usually understood as the seat, not just of our feelings and passions, but of our mind and will as well. The lev is where we uncover our deepest commitments and values, what we are willing to fight and even die for. That is why we are commanded to "love Adonai your God with all your heart" (Deuteronomy 6:5).

For Resh Lakish, study, teaching, and "mixing it up" with other religious scholars were at the very center of his vocation and life. Engagement with others (in the spirit of mutual respect) was a primary activity of the dialogical tradition that he was a part of. But like any warrior, he played for keeps, and we can only imagine this former gladiator engaged in impassioned debates with his colleagues on issues of law, practice, life, and death. He surely must have come across to his rabbinic peers as a person who could "move mountains"—not literally, but with his fiery pugnacity, intensity, and tenacity.

———————————

I recall a time in my life when I was tempted to give up, to walk away from something that I loved very much. As I think back on it today, stamina was the only thing that got me through the experience. I've discussed at some length the role that the martial arts have played in my own spiritual development, and how they can help us—either through their practice or their principles—strive to become warriors of the soul.

In my very traditional Shotokan karate system, you can only test for your black belt once a year—and it usually takes five or six years before your instructors will even allow you to participate in the exam, which takes place at the very end of a special training retreat. I'd put in those many years of practice, and my time had come to stand before my senior instructors and demonstrate my abilities as a karate practitioner. I was anxious, excited, and highly motivated. After half a decade of discipline, training, and knowing my place in the pecking order, I felt ready to be evaluated by my teachers.

By the time special training was over, I was exhausted, drained on every level of my being. I have come to see now, years later, how that was the point of placing the black belt exam at the end of our retreat. How do you test to see if someone truly has heart? You evaluate them not at the start of our practice, when everybody is fresh, but at the end, when most of us are about to collapse and want nothing more than to go home and sleep. Who can push *past* their limits? Who can reach deep within themselves and successfully retrieve whatever remnants are left in their reservoirs of passion, skill, and determination? Who can uncover and display their lev, their innermost character and commitment?

After having trained regularly and intensively for a year to perform at my peak level and try to pass my exam, I gave it my best. I, along with the other black belt candidates, spent most of the day being observed on how well we performed in three key areas: basic techniques, forms, and sparring. At the end of the day, when the senior instructors called out the names of those who had been promoted, my name was not on the list. I had failed to pass. It's hard to describe how despondent I felt after having put in so much time and effort, and having my desire thwarted. I would have to wait an entire year, according to the rules of my system, before I could try for my black belt again.

The days and weeks that followed were filled with self-pity and self-doubt. I wanted to quit. What more did my teachers want from me, and how much harder could I train? With the passage of some time, I knew that I couldn't give up. I'd put too much of myself into karate, and it had given me back so much in return. One of those gifts was humility; I had to accept the fact that in the judgment of my senior instructors, I just wasn't yet ready for my black belt. That knowledge hurt, but it also propelled me forward. I had faith in myself—in my skills and my heart—and I regained the desire to continue my training. If I couldn't get past this blow to my ego, I didn't belong on the dojo floor.

"I'm glad you didn't take the easy way out, like so many others," one of my favorite teachers told me. "You just have to jump right back onto that horse and start riding again. The trail hasn't gone anywhere." While I had instructors to help me and to guide me by their example, it was absolutely clear to me that I had to overcome this challenge alone—of my own initiative, and harnessing my own powers of resiliency.

I passed the exam the following year and earned my black belt.

GO FORTH

The guidance and support of others can be essential as we strive to overcome life's obstacles. In the end, though, we alone are the final arbiters of the paths we take and the choices we make. Jean-Paul Sartre claims that we are "condemned" to this freedom; others believe that it is in the decision-making process itself—

that place of ambiguity where nothing is certain yet all is possible—that we as human beings find our highest natures. If we do not want that freedom to atrophy, it must be exercised, like a muscle, again and again. Each conscious moment presents us with a multiplicity of options, a maze of alternatives. How we choose to face and respond to them shapes our souls and directs our steps, and makes us models for those who follow us.

Abraham faces a choice of his own in the Mesopotamian town of Haran, a name that means "crossroads." Not only does the biblical patriarch (a revered figure in Judaism, Christianity, and Islam) receive a divine call at the crossroads of his life—he receives it at a turning point in the Bible itself. Many scholars consider Abraham the first major historical figure in the book of Genesis. Unlike his predecessors Adam and Noah, who seem to be symbols or representations woven into ancient myths, Abraham comes across as a *person*, not a persona; he is an identifiable human being who lives in a specific place and at a particular time. While we know nothing about Abraham's character when he initially appears, we do know that God selects him to fulfill a sacred and significant mission. God gives Abraham (known at this early stage as Abram) a charge: "Go forth from your native land, and from your father's house, to the land that I will show you. And I will make of you a great nation, and I will bless you" (Genesis 12:1–2).

Although God's words take the form of a command, Abraham does not have to accept the mission. In fact, other characters in the Bible flee from such divine charges. And God doesn't seem to want to make this choice very easy for the patriarch. Is it really necessary for God to remind Abraham that he must give up so much—his homeland, his hearth, his way of life—in order to venture into the unknown? Why doesn't God just say, "Go to the land that I will show you," without any additional comment? Very likely, in my view, to suggest that what Abraham is about to embark on is not a "trip" but a trial, a test—the first of many he must encounter, and endure, throughout his life.

Abraham does choose to accept the celestial charge. With his family in tow, he begins the difficult pilgrimage, traveling across the deserts of Mesopotamia to Canaan, from Canaan down to Egypt, and then from Egypt back to what will become known as the Promised Land. The fact that Abraham gives up everything that is comfortable and familiar for the ambiguity of a promised but as yet unrealized future affords us a glimpse of the confidence and stamina he will display more overtly later in the story. These qualities will help him to surmount the challenges and hardships that await him.

Soon after he is more settled, Abraham learns that God intends to destroy the cities and inhabitants of Sodom and Gomorrah as punishment for their sinful behavior. With the courage and sense of purpose that one would expect from a spiritual warrior, he confronts God directly and questions the divine plan: "Abraham came forward and said, 'Will you sweep away the innocent along with the guilty? What if there should be fifty innocent within the city; will you then wipe out the place and not forgive it for the sake of the innocent fifty who are in it? Far be it from you to do such a thing, to bring death upon the innocent as well as the guilty, so that innocent and guilty fare alike. Far be it from you! Shall not the judge of all the earth deal justly?'" (Genesis 18:23–25).

Abraham utilizes the weapons of logic, negotiation, and even guilt—along with a plea for mercy—in a forceful attempt to dissuade God from proceeding with the annihilation. Since God permitted a saving remnant after the flood (owing to the righteousness of Noah), why not apply the same rationale to this situation? If God tested Abraham in Haran, their roles seem reversed here—Abraham appears to be testing *God*. Is the Creator judging fairly and consistently? Does the divine value system have proper boundaries? How evolved is God's capacity for compassion? God agrees not to destroy the population if fifty innocent people can be found. Yet Abraham steps forward once again to protect any potential innocents: "Abraham spoke up again, saying, 'Here I am presuming to speak to the Lord, I who am but dust and ashes: What if the fifty innocent should lack five? Will you destroy the whole city for want of the five?' And

God answered, 'I will not destroy it if I find forty-five there'"
(Genesis 18:27–28).

Abraham continues to stand his ground. As far as the patriarch is concerned, he is engaged in a battle against injustice, and
he will not give up the fight—regardless of the impossible odds
and surpassing power of his divine "adversary." Abraham's self-
deprecating words are just a mask for his resolute and tenacious
will. Returning to his argument, he asks God if the same rule
would apply if forty innocent people could be found, and God
says the city will still be spared for the sake of the forty. Then
Abraham says, "Let the Lord not be angry if I go on: What if
thirty should be found there?" (Genesis 18:30). God agrees to
spare the city for the sake of the thirty. As a result of his courage,
confidence, and persistent refusal to take no for an answer, Abraham is able to reduce the number of innocents who would save
the other inhabitants of the city to just ten, at which point the
negotiations come to an end. Yet not even those ten souls can be
discovered in antiquity's most notorious den of iniquity, and the
residents of Sodom and Gomorrah are finally consumed by fire
and sulfur that descend from the sky.

Abraham's bold tenacity when confronted by trials and his
willingness to challenge others—and himself—are character
traits that become especially relevant and valuable later in the
Genesis narrative. In a section referred to as the Akedah, or "the
Binding," Abraham tries to sacrifice his son, Isaac, to God. The
patriarch attempts this dreadful act not because he wants to, but
because it is what God orders him to do—it is an act of will, not
an expression of desire. And since the text highlights how much
Abraham loves his son, his external behavior may very well stand
in polar opposition to his internal emotions. Abraham wakes at
dawn, begins a three-day journey, and eventually arrives at the
divinely appointed spot where the sacrifice is to occur. He builds
an altar, lays out firewood, binds Isaac, and lifts a knife. Just
then, "an angel of the Lord called to him from heaven: 'Abraham! Abraham!' And he answered, 'Here I am.' And he said,
'Lay not your hand against the boy, nor do the least thing to

him. For now I know that you fear God, since you have not withheld your own beloved son from me'" (Genesis 22:11–12). Abraham sees a ram caught in a nearby thicket and offers it instead of Isaac.

This disturbing episode has raised many vexing questions for centuries, but one thing that is never questioned is the resolve that Abraham shows as he attempts to fulfill God's command. Though some commentators (such as Maimonides) argue that Abraham grasped the charge was really just a test of faith from the outset and that the patriarch—knowing full well that he would not have to kill his son in the end—was merely going through the motions in order to pass it, the Bible itself is silent on the subject. Abraham speaks very little during all of this, but if he *did* truly believe that this was a task God required of him, we can only imagine the emotional pain he would have had to endure. Yet endure it he does, responding to God's challenge by challenging himself.

When Abraham responds to the angel's call by saying, "Here I am," he uses a Hebrew word (*Hineni*) that has a coded meaning in the Jewish tradition. For the rabbis, *Hineni* has often been viewed as a signifier that points to a person of moral and spiritual rectitude, an individual who is ready and able to follow the divine will. It is a word uttered by Jacob, Moses, Samuel, and Isaiah, an expression that conveys an unrelenting commitment to their sacred calling, despite its challenges. Abraham's great strength resides in this stamina of spirit, his ability to endure the often difficult relationship he has with God. Since any meaningful relationship involves risks, tests, and developing a capacity to be present for the other person, Abraham is a role model for all of us.

THE LORD AND THE RING

Not all callings may seem sacred to us. Nevertheless, if even questionable vocations can lead toward new insights, emotional maturity, and spiritual growth, there is a value in them that should not be denied—certainly for the practitioner involved.

Ray "Boom Boom" Mancini is a man imbued with a deep spirituality yet haunted by ever-present demons from his past, a former world champion boxer who frequently seems more aware of his own internal battles than those with his prior opponents. While he is now retired, Mancini was once a fierce competitor and a dangerous brawler. Today he comes across more like an impassioned preacher.

I spoke with Mancini about the link between spirituality and being a fighter:

"People used to ask me, 'What were you thinking and doing between rounds?' I said I was praying. I'd say, 'Oh, God, give me the strength to get through this round.' Every round is a separate fight. When you're going fifteen rounds, you don't think of all fifteen rounds—if you think about all fifteen rounds before you get in there, you get overwhelmed. So you got fifteen separate fights, and you just worry about getting through each one. When I went into a fight, I didn't pray for a win. I'd pray for the strength to get through it, to do my best. I knew if I did my best, if I had the strength to get through, I'd be successful. And I'd pray that nobody would get seriously hurt.

"I knew that if I was paying my dues and doing things correctly," Mancini continued, "that if I got beat it was because my opponent was just better than me that night, not because I beat myself. That's actually the one thing I'm the most proud of as a former boxer and also as a man—when people ask me what was my greatest strength, I say my greatest strength was my strength of mind. You go to war with yourself and your demons before you go to war with your opponent, before the bout even begins."

Mancini told me that he's had two profoundly spiritual experiences in his life, both of which were connected with his career as a professional fighter. The first was winning the world title. "It was a euphoric feeling," he said. I asked him what made it *spiritual,* why it was any different from simply experiencing a rush of adrenaline.

"I'd already got a shot at it once and I wasn't successful," answered Mancini. "I didn't think I'd ever get another. I said, 'God, whatever your plan is, I want to win this title for my father. Please just give me this opportunity to get it for him.' When I went into the ring, that was the one fight when I felt completely at peace. I was confident and at peace. I was nervous, sure, but I somehow felt that it was going to be my day."

Lenny Mancini, Ray's father, had been his great inspiration and the driving force in his career. Lenny had himself been a top-ranked lightweight contender in the 1940s, but after he was wounded during the Second World War, his dream was shattered. Ray took it upon himself to fulfill that dream, to bring a world championship belt to the Mancini household. After he knocked out Arturo Frias with a flurry of punches during the first round of their title fight on May 8, 1982, Mancini became the world champion.

But it wasn't just prayer, or the sense of fulfilling his destiny, that made winning the world title a spiritual experience for Mancini. It was also the fact that it transported him to a different realm: "You have to take your mind to a different place, to a higher place. You've got to overcome the pain and anything that is going to try to stop you, any disappointment or roadblock that gets in the way. You have to take your mind to a different place or it's not gonna happen. And if you get that pain or get hurt, you take your mind, you focus on a place of peace, you don't let anything else overcome that."

We turned to the subject of the accident—the greatest tragedy of his life, yet an event Mancini considers the second most spiritual experience he's ever gone through. The accident took place during Mancini's second title defense against a South Korean boxer named Deuk-Koo Kim. Mancini squared off against the formidable contender in a sold-out Caesar's Palace on November 13, 1982. The scheduled fifteen-round fight was extremely tight—too close to call—and when the fighters entered the fourteenth round, it became a vicious brawl. Yet before the bell could sound and force a final round, Mancini knocked out Kim with a series of powerful and devastating punches to the head—and Kim collapsed onto the canvas. He could not be revived and was immediately taken to a hospital. Kim died from severe brain injuries four days later.

One week after Kim's death, the two boxers appeared on the cover of *Sports Illustrated* under the caption, "Tragedy in the Ring." Within four months of this tragedy, both Kim's mother and the match's referee had committed suicide. As a result of this horrific accident, all of the professional boxing associations reduced the total number of rounds in title fights from fifteen to twelve. Many argued that the sport be banned. Mancini fell into a deep depression.

I asked him whether the event and its immediate fallout changed him professionally and/or personally:

"Well, both," Mancini said. "How could it not? When I started fighting, I wanted to be world champion for my father. I fought for righteous reasons. And I would have fought for nothing to win the world title. Literally, I would have. But after that wonderful moment, it had become a business to me. After the Kim fight there was nothing righteous about it anymore. It just took all the love and everything righteous about it away."

Mancini attended Kim's funeral in South Korea and resolved to continue with his boxing career. It was one of the most difficult decisions of his life.

"I prayed a lot about it," he said. "My hometown priest helped me. I said, 'Father Tim, help me. What would you do?' He said, 'Ray, I can't answer that. That's a question you're going to have to answer and you're going to have to do it through prayer.' He said look, I was put here on this earth, I have a gift, I was put here for a reason. He said as a priest they come to him and he's there for them. He says he gives hope to others. He says *I* give hope to others, to Youngstown, Ohio. He says the people in this town look at you, they live vicariously through you. God gave you that gift, put you here for that reason. He says if he should decide to leave the priesthood, he'd be denying those people his own gift—just like if I retired I'd be denying those people my gift. But he says this is something you're gonna have to go through and figure out on your own. You gotta pray about it and open your heart and listen for the answer, and it'll be the right answer."

The spirituality of the experience was in Mancini's journey through the darkness, a journey he had to make alone. I asked him how he was able to move on.

"I didn't take a long time to get back into the ring," Mancini notes. "I know myself. I had to move on with my life. I had to come to grips with things, to accept the reality of the situation and to grow from it and evolve. I tend to deal with things right away and move on quickly, because if I let them linger I'll never get moving. That fight with Kim happened in November and I got back in the ring in February because I had to move on, I just had to. That's the only way. I couldn't bring Kim back. I wished I could have, but I'm not God. I couldn't change what happened. I decided to move forward with my career, and the reason I did is because I just felt that I have a world title for my father and now I wanted an opportunity to get my financial security for me and my family, and you know, God forbid, I thought, if I'm gonna lose a title I want to lose it in the ring. I don't want to give it up, walk away. I want to lose it in the ring like a fighter."

How did he find the inner strength to endure the pain and the guilt, I asked him. Was it prayer and faith alone that helped him make it through the experience?

"I got a letter," Mancini responded, "from a sixth-grade elementary school class from Italy, and they said, 'Ray Mancini, we know that you're going through a very difficult time and we pray for you. We hope that you will come back and come back stronger,' and all these nice things, but I remember, especially, one thing they said—we know that God lets those really challenging things happen only to those who are strong enough to handle them, and we know that you are a very strong man and that you will be able to handle it and you will move on, you'll move forward with even more force and spirit in your life. That letter was so inspirational. I was blown away by it."

I noted that muscles only grow and toughen through working out, through breaking down the muscle tissue so that it grows back stronger than before. I asked Mancini if he thought that dynamic can be applied to our souls. Do we grow through toil and sweat and blood? Can we find spirituality and inner growth through struggle and pain?

"Oh, absolutely," Mancini responded without hesitation. "I think that's the only way you find it. Because when it's rosy out there, what do we need to rely on our faith for? Life's a bowl of cherries, life's great, man, you know, sunshine—no. You grow through sticking with the pain and suffering. I think that's the only way, because if you don't understand pain and suffering, how can you know what the other side is?"

FIGHT OR FLIGHT

We've looked at the lives and lessons of boxers and gladiators, black belts and special agents, mystics and monks. The biographies of spiritual warriors are diverse. Yet the goals of these men and women—empowerment, transformation, redemption—are the same. As we have seen, you don't need to be a physical fighter (or a metaphysical prophet) to follow the path of the spiritual warrior. What you need, perhaps more than any of the other principles that we have explored, is a relentless drive to transcend adversity. Without the will to persist and evolve, we will stay lost in our dark forests.

A warrior is not afraid to face adversity. He or she fully grasps that our attempts at evasion, avoidance, and denial will ultimately never succeed as the human condition bounces us from one challenge to the next. It is one thing to restrain yourself from an opponent (an idea that we will discuss in the next chapter and the next step on the warrior's path), and it is quite another to fall into the trap of escapism. When we try to run away from struggle and pain, we paradoxically do ourselves more harm than good.

Like a flower stem when it finally breaks through soil, our souls are often forged through trial and toil. That is what makes them stronger, more open, and able to bloom. Stamina and endurance are tools that can support and carry us through life's hardships.

———————

At times, studying the behavior of even nonhuman forms of life can help us to better understand and improve ourselves and the world around us. That is what led Konrad Lorenz, through observing the actions of animals, to his famous description of the "fight or flight" response. He found that when an animal is threatened (either by another animal or by a pack of them), it almost always chooses between one of two alternatives: to fight for its life, or to flee for it. One of the most compelling and indelible photographs I have ever seen shows a baboon being attacked by a much larger cheetah. I first saw the picture as a child in an anthology of photos from old *Life* magazine essays. It is an action shot, out of focus and very grainy, but the raw terror in the baboon's eyes is clear—as is the fact that it is going to lose the confrontation and, ultimately, its life.

The baboon, unable to outrun the cheetah and with nowhere else to turn, reels to face the great cat. Its mouth agape as if in a scream, the baboon looks as if it is about to trip over its own legs. The expression in its wildly protruding eyes is one of desperation, but also one of defiance. I have always viewed that baboon as the visual epitome of the fight response, the bold, last-ditch effort of a living being to lash out against its fate.

There are powerful parallels in human behavior. When we feel cornered, or when all seems lost, we often panic and lash out at the wrong targets, or when we shouldn't strike at all. What differentiates humans—especially those among us who are the most evolved—from other animals is our capacity to respond to conflict in less primal and potentially destructive ways. We can engage in dialogue, negotiate with our adversary, and at times come to a rational compromise. We can exercise patience and fortitude.

Humans also share the second response to distress that is common in animals: flight. While animals flee from predators or competitors out of a biological instinct for self-preservation, human beings frequently try to run away, not only from challenges and obstacles, but when we *ourselves* have become our own enemies. For that, we need a measure of self-awareness, not just of our physical selves, but of our moral and spiritual selves as well, that seems unmatched in the rest of the animal kingdom. That's the good news. The bad news is that, despite our gift of self-awareness, the flight impulse can drive us to make damaging, fear-based choices, directing us not to empowerment but enslavement.

Spiritual warriors are not motivated to take action merely to save their own skin. Self-transcendence, not self-preservation, is the mission behind their method. Yet none of their work, or ours, can happen without faith—faith not just in our own abilities, but in a higher power. Sometimes it is only after hitting rock bottom that we find this hidden capacity, that we discover that, irrespective of the obstacles we must all inevitably confront and endure, life has value and meaning. But why would a transcendent force allow for such tribulation? Why not intervene and prevent the fall from occurring in the first place? Because as mortal beings, we need to come to that realization ourselves— the knowledge that we are only human, that we are flawed, that there is (if we open our souls and allow it entry) something greater that will lovingly guide us through our struggles and challenges. That "something greater" is God. Which leaves us with two options: we can grope for a way out alone, or we can strive to endure our hardships and have faith that our divine partner will ultimately lead us to safety.

7

FORCE WITHOUT FEROCITY

SINCE EXPERIENCES OF struggle and challenge can help to develop, rather than diminish, the soul of a spiritual warrior, wouldn't we want to be in a state of perpetual confrontation and engagement? Wouldn't we, in order to strengthen our inner lives, want to constantly seek out new, ever more daunting contests? Although it may seem counterintuitive at first, direct engagement is not always the best path for a warrior to take in a particular situation. With the proper training and mindset, it is often possible to end a battle before it has even begun, to neutralize opponents (perhaps even our own internal adversaries) before they can cause harm to us or we can cause harm to them.

A spiritual warrior knows when to use the quality of *restraint* as a powerful weapon—not just to surmount obstacles, but to enlarge and enrich our own souls.

This is a foundational principle in most martial arts systems. According to Master Funakoshi: "To win one hundred victories in one hundred battles does not prove superior skill; rather, to

defeat the enemy without fighting indicates superior skill."
Sometimes it takes more courage, and demonstrates more skill,
to refrain from engaging with an opponent rather than to engage with one. How, then, do we measure "defeat" and "victory"
in concrete terms? When we act out of our baser impulses, when
we fight when we really don't need to—these are expressions of
weakness, not strength. A seasoned and fully evolved warrior
knows when to use his or her full force against an adversary, and
when such extreme action is unnecessary—or even unwar-
ranted—in a given context.

Whether in combat or in life, less can very frequently be
more. Holding back our power is not the equivalent of giving
up. Far from it. It can be our gateway to progress.

RESTRAINT AND PATIENCE

About midway through my years as a rabbinical student, while
I was living in New York, I experienced a breakup with a girl-
friend I cared very deeply about. Although both of us had come
to the realization that we weren't meant to be together, I was still
crushed. All of the feelings and memories from my earlier, painful breakup with the Princeton woman flooded over me anew.
Do I fight for her anyway? No, that would be foolish. Do I
choose the other option and flee? I knew I had to do something
to try to heal my heart again, and I was hearing the call of the
wild, as I often did in times of distress. My summer vacation was
getting close and I had no solid plans yet. A dude ranch would
be the answer and my salve, I told myself, and it had to be one
somewhere in Montana.

Why Montana? Though Alaska had served as my personal
Sinai, the place where I had experienced some of the most spiritual and revelatory moments in my life (dogsledding above the
Arctic Circle, witnessing the majesty of the northern lights, and
other events and encounters that I've written about in other
books), the Big Sky State was the site of my first student pulpit,
a small congregation in the town of Butte. I got to know the

mountains and forests in and around Butte, and during my monthly visits I always tried to take time for myself to sojourn around the state. Its beauty soothed me.

I called my friend Randy, who was able to arrange everything for me. Randy lived in Butte, and we'd developed our friendship while I was his community's student rabbi. In addition to being the synagogue's president at the time of my tenure, he also happened to be a professional travel agent. I simply told Randy that I wanted to stay at a no-frills, old-school dude ranch, right in the heart of the Rockies. Within days, he'd found what he said was the perfect place, made my reservation, and booked my flights. A few weeks later, when the semester ended, I packed my bags and took an airplane to Great Falls.

During my year of serving Butte's Jewish community, I'd been to most of Montana's other major cities: Billings, Missoula, Helena, and Bozeman. When I landed in Great Falls and saw a silly and decrepit stuffed grizzly on display in the airport's terminal, I decided that it was one city I could probably afford to skip. I met my driver, one of the wranglers from the dude ranch, in a battered pick-up. We drove west toward the tiny town of Augusta, less than an hour from Great Falls. After only about thirty minutes of driving, the Rocky Mountains seemed to rise up and stand just for me as they started to come into view. I was back in Big Sky country, far away from the scene of the crime.

We passed Augusta (with its single bar, convenience store, and sporting goods shop) and turned onto a gravel road that led directly into the mountains. Soon we'd entered a valley and drove along Ford Creek for another several minutes before we reached our final destination. The ranch, which straddled the creek, was situated in the Lewis and Clark National Forest and flanked by rugged mountains. It was also located at the confluence of both the Bob Marshall Wilderness and the Scapegoat Wilderness, remote areas of spectacular beauty that were rich with wildlife such as elk, deer, and eagles.

At the ranch, I stayed in a rustic log cabin for a week and rode horses every day. At night I ate in the dining tent with the other guests, but mostly I kept to myself. The routine alone helped me to relax and forget about my heartbreak. Early each morning, I put on my cowboy boots, entered the corral, and chose a horse. I developed relationships with most of the wranglers (and I noticed a very pretty one, the only woman among the crew, on the day of my arrival). They were young and very friendly, and they were the ones who'd accompany me along the various trails. After saddling up the horse with me, the wrangler would then become my guide, and the two of us would set out on the day's excursion.

Some of the trails were extremely steep, even a bit treacherous at points, but each one was breathtaking. I rode through pine trees and canyons, meadows and grasslands; I passed alpine lakes, trout streams, waterfalls, and wildflowers. When possible, my guide and I would gallop over the flatlands. All around us, of course, were stunning vistas, and we stopped often to take in the views. I recall the summit of one mountain trail in particular. It had been a difficult ride, and our horses were tired. As the wrangler took care of our animals, I walked to the edge of the summit and found a boulder to sit on. The view was astounding. If I looked east, I could see the vast and wide-open Montana plains, unfolding forever like a carpet of grass and earth. If I turned to face west, the snow-capped peaks of the Continental Divide loomed in front of me. Despite the wind, the cold, and the pain, I'd been given a glimpse of heaven, a refuge to nurse my wounds.

Late one afternoon, after I'd returned from a ride, I struck up a conversation with the woman from the corral. She was on a break. As we sat on the porch of my cabin and tossed a Frisbee to one of the dogs on the property, she told me about working as a wrangler and ranch hand that summer, how she was from Salt Lake City, and how she had been raised in a repressive Mormon household that she was now trying to break away from. Surprised at how much she was sharing with a total stranger, I asked her if the owner allowed her to mingle with the guests. "I couldn't care less," she said with a wave of her hand. "Besides," she went on with a smirk, "I saw that you were looking at me."

We agreed to meet later that night, after she had finished her work. *Is this kosher?* I wondered. But I didn't really care, either. I had come to Montana to get over my ex-girlfriend. I wanted to heal my heart through the beauty of the mountains, and I was doing just that. Since the opportunity to find additional comfort through another woman had suddenly presented itself to me, why shouldn't I embrace this newfound situation?

And thus we began our tryst. It was fun until the day we went fly-fishing.

It was hot, and she was wearing shorts. As I knelt down to pick up a fly I'd dropped near the creek, I saw that her legs were covered with cuts. I'd noted a few things during the brief period we were with each other that struck me as unusual and gave me some pause (such as her clinginess to somebody she barely knew), but I ignored any reservations I had about her because I was having a good time, because I was focused only on my own desires and on overcoming my personal pain. Why should I restrain myself and deprive myself of pleasure? Yet now I knew there was something very wrong with her, and very wrong about the entire situation. I asked her about the cuts.

"Oh, I just take a razor blade to myself from time to time," she responded. "It's become a habit."

I'd had enough pastoral training and common sense by that point to recognize a person with serious psychological and emotional problems.

"You know, you're really hurting yourself," I said. "Are you getting help?"

The two of us sat by the creek and talked about her many issues. She told me about the medication she was taking for her bipolar disorder, about her abusive father, about her struggle with her sexual orientation. She told me that she was aware of how confused and needy she was at this stage in her life, and that she hoped working at the dude ranch over the summer might help her to figure things out. "We can still hang out, right?" she asked. "I have a therapist back in Salt Lake. I don't see any harm in this."

I did. While my lust still wanted her, I now had knowledge about this troubled woman that made holding back a moral imperative; otherwise, I'd be taking advantage of a fragile, struggling soul. I'd acted irresponsibly. I'd *used* someone selfishly and without restraint, and I'd been too preoccupied with satisfying my own needs to pick up on the gravity of hers at the outset of our relationship. I apologized to her for starting something that I didn't think was right or healthy for either one of us. All I could offer her was my friendship.

I learned an extremely valuable lesson from that experience. Restraint can be difficult, even when we sense that a situation requires it. In certain contexts, when we unleash a desire rather than set a boundary, mistakes are inevitable. I also learned how vital patience is, both in helping us to use sound judgment and in the evolution of our characters. I erred in that area, too. I should have waited for my heart to mend a bit more before jumping into anything with a woman, and because I didn't, because I acted out of impulsivity and *im*patience, I was culpable for having caused a potential injury to another human being. Patience is more than a virtue—it's a tool for maturity and growth.

It can, in some situations, be even more of a challenge for us—and require more strength and force of will—to *refrain* from acting when all of our passions and desires are driving us to do so. I experienced that psychic tug-of-war myself in the mountains of Montana, and, as I've just described, I failed the test. A spiritual warrior understands the power of both restraint and its interrelated counterpart, patience. We see this power clearly, not just on the field of combat, but especially in our own interpersonal relationships.

Listen to the following words from Resh Lakish, as transcribed in the Talmud fifteen hundred years ago: "The instruction of the young should not be interrupted, even by the building of the Temple [itself]." While Resh Lakish and the other Talmudic sages lived several centuries after the destruction of the Second Temple in Jerusalem by the Romans in 70 C.E., their yearning for its restoration and reconsecration was intense. To this day, many Jewish traditionalists still pray for the rebuilding of the Holy Temple. For some (Jew and Christian alike) it would be a sign we have entered the messianic era.

That is what makes this teaching from Resh Lakish so radical, and so representative of the way a spiritual warrior should approach life in general. To argue that the nurturing of our youth should take precedence over everything, even the most sacred of activities, that our own needs and desires—however valid they may be—must be subordinate to those of our children, is a daring and audacious idea. If a warrior's mission is to protect and guide others, then our focus can never be primarily on ourselves. That would be narcissism, the soul's nemesis. We must restrain our own yearnings. We must exercise patience. And we must always value human beings, as images of the divine, over edifices and icons. Even if that means the Messiah will have to wait as a consequence.

CONTRACTION

As we grow in confidence, stamina, and strength, we have to use our judgment as to when, and how, to best use those capacities. Just because we are powerful doesn't mean we have to exercise that power. In fact, this chapter has highlighted ways in which holding back our power and passion, when faced with a challenge, can yield some wonderful outcomes. Taking a step back, withdrawing or withholding a part of ourselves, is not just an effective technique for handling adversity and hardship; it can also serve as a tool to transform our souls, to lead us toward even greater self-empowerment and stronger, more mature relationships with others—including with the *highest* of powers.

In chapter 5, we explored the mystical teachings of Rabbi Isaac Luria, particularly his concept of tzimtzum (withdrawal or contraction) as it related to the creation of the world. According to Lurianic Kabbalah, as we discussed, primeval existence was saturated with the all-enveloping presence of divinity, and there was no space for anything else—not heaven, earth, the seas, or living beings. In order for the world to come into being, God had to "withdraw," or step back, to make room for it.

Luria's interpretation of the moment of creation is radically different from the description in the first verses of the book of Genesis. But another, later mystic, Rabbi Dov Baer of Mezeritch (who died in 1772), took Luria's daring idea even further, applying it not only to the interaction between God and the world, but to our relationships with other people. For this important Hasidic master, tzimtzum was the key not to understanding the secrets of the universe, but to unlocking the mysteries of interpersonal dynamics.

Dov Baer, also known as the Great Maggid, offers the following parable to show us how contraction can lead to connection, how holding back can paradoxically reveal:

> A parable about a rabbi who teaches his student: If the student trembles at the words of his rabbi, and inclines his heart toward these words, [then] the rabbi is able to reveal, and open for him, the doors to the gates of wisdom, even though he will not be able to teach him all of his great and mighty wisdom. . . . Thus [the rabbi] needs to "shrink" his own wisdom so that it will be [rendered] comprehensible to the student.

For the Maggid, the only way that a pupil will be able to begin to grasp the teachings of his rabbi is through a twofold process. First, he must respect, perhaps even revere his mentor, and thus become receptive to his message; second, there must be an act of tzimtzum—in this case, the contraction, or "shrinkage," of the rabbi's wisdom. What the rabbi shows him is merely the threshold, the "doors to the gates" of his knowledge; the rabbi must first filter, or mediate, the intensity of his wisdom if any real intellectual contact is to occur between teacher and student. The motivation for this act of contraction is love, like the love of a father for his son. And that is exactly the analogy the

Maggid uses next, utilizing the imagery of the angels that were created for the ark of the covenant:

> It is written, "and you shall make two cherubim [*keruvim*]." (Exodus 25:18) As our sages interpret the word, *keravya* [a play on the Hebrew phrase *ke-ravya*, "like an infant"]. This is meant to explain the way of the father who, because of his love for the child, distorts his speech and speaks in the manner of a child, or contracts his intellect into that of the child. We therefore find that the father is able to reach the level of [the intellect of] the son, and that explains the verse, "and you shall make two cherubim."

The rabbi contracts the full extent of his wisdom, and the father holds back and carefully selects his words, out of a desire both to connect with their younger, less experienced counterparts and to impart knowledge that is graspable. Each one "comes down" to the level of the recipient so as to protect and not overwhelm him. A professor of neuroscience wouldn't attempt to lecture a freshmen chemistry student on his latest scholarly work; the commander of a Delta Force unit wouldn't try to explain how to insert and extract a strike team to a brand new soldier who hadn't yet gone through basic training. Despite natural and inevitable imbalances in age, experience, knowledge, and power (in its broadest sense), "contraction" makes connection and communication between human beings possible. Why? Because it functions as a filter and a mediating force, and it allows people at very different places in life to interact with one another.

The mission of a spiritual warrior is to protect and guide others—especially those who are vulnerable and/or in need—and not only to cultivate his or her own capabilities. The contact and interpersonal relationship that tzimtzum allows for is unique and invaluable, in that it helps *both* people involved in the dynamic to evolve and grow, irrespective of their current level of development. The paradox of tzimtzum is that it empowers our souls while necessitating that we refrain from fully exercising that power.

Rabbi Isaac Luria described the role that contraction played when God created the world. The Maggid moves beyond interactions between people and explains how we who dwell in the world can use the same technique for relating to, and connecting with, God. We have learned that God had to withdraw in order for the divine-human relationship to occur, so that we would have the space in which to exist. But the goal of a mystic is not mere existence—it is interconnection and intimacy with his or her Creator.

When, in the face of God's overwhelming and ungraspable infinity, we ourselves perform tzimtzum (and become "as nothing," in the words of the Maggid), then, like the merger of two bodies of water, we are able to merge with God. This is communion, the most profound kind of relationship. What at the surface seems like an act of concealment is, at the highest of spiritual levels, actually an act of disclosure and revelation. Mystical communion involves both contact and communication, and neither one is possible through direct channels. The path to God is a path of *in*direction, paradox, and mystery.

It is our own ego, as is so often the case, that is the primary adversary in this process, the impediment to an improved soul and to solid relationships. Only when we can conceive of ourselves "as nothing" can the dynamic of contraction take place. And then, once we have transcended ourselves, will we finally be able to find our best selves.

BE ALL YOU CAN BE

You don't need to be a mystic in a flowing white robe in order to become a warrior of the spirit. We all can potentially attain this level of achievement, whether we are accountants, cooks, or homemakers. Moreover, our internal capability as an evolved warrior might not always be visible to the outside world—nor can it be judged by the world. There is an insightful Hasidic story that expresses these ideas very compellingly:

When Rabbi Zusya lay on his deathbed, his disciples crowded around him and asked what frightened him as he pondered having to soon stand before the High Court in Heaven. The rabbi replied, "I am not afraid that they will say to me, Zusya, why were you not more like Moses, our great teacher? Rather, I am fearful that they will ask, Zusya, why were you not more like Zusya?"

We cannot, and should not, compare our paths or our progress with those of others. The driving force of our lives and work ought to be the quest to live up to the best that is within each and every one of us. That is the warrior's noble, sacred mission.

Yet in order to grow and gain, we must sometimes restrain. In chapter 1, I referred to the work of Søren Kierkegaard (1813–1855), the Danish existentialist philosopher. He argued that only through our willingness to make a leap into uncertainty and adopting an attitude of "infinite resignation" as to our capacity to understand an ineffable, transcendent God would we be able to evolve as spiritual beings. For Kierkegaard, reeling in our confidence and trust in reason is a key stage on the path to true faith, for only through such an attitude can we become aware of our own "eternal validity." As I explained in that chapter, Kierkegaard's spiritual system is—despite appearances to the contrary—active rather than passive, a manifestation of strength and courage, not weakness and fear. It is a humble spirituality, but also an assertive and forceful one, a powerful affirmation (through acceptance) of our limited humanity.

Some important biographical details will help us to better grasp Kierkegaard's view about what constitutes a spiritual warrior, or what he calls a "knight of faith." Kierkegaard was born in Copenhagen to a wealthy and devout Lutheran father. The future philosopher and theologian began his studies at Copenhagen University in 1830 at the age of seventeen. As a student, he lived a life of unrestrained self-indulgence, drinking, and debauching along with his friends—a life very different from the one of discipline and self-transcendence he would later advocate as a religious writer. Despite his years of aimless carousing and his embrace of secular living (and perhaps owing to his background in a stern and observant Lutheran household), Kierkegaard still embarked on occasional forays into the world of formalized, normative religion and worship.

Little happened for him in the context of church, which he saw as presenting a bourgeois, sentimental, and irrelevant form of Christianity. Yet we know from his journals that something transformative occurred on May 18, 1838, something that would alter his life and worldview forever: Kierkegaard experienced a deep spiritual epiphany. It isn't clear what triggered this profound event, but from that day on Kierkegaard would never be the same. As he wrote soon after this life-changing experience, "I mean to labor to achieve a far more inward relation to Christianity; hitherto I have fought for its truth while in a sense standing outside it." Kierkegaard was now ready to step into the ring.

The reality of a transcendent God, a God who is untouchable, elusive, beyond us, rests at the very heart of Kierkegaard's theology. Georg Wilhelm Friedrich Hegel and many other post-Renaissance thinkers had advocated the idea of a God who was immanent in history and omnipresent in human experience. Hegel argued that God (or the "Infinite Spirit") was manifest in the material, extant world, not separate from it. This position was anathema to Kierkegaard, who claimed that there was a "deep gulf of qualitative difference" between the finite and the Infinite. While humanity is ensconced in the realm of existence, God, the divine Other, dwells in the sphere of the limitless and the eternal, absolutely independent of the world. We are different from God not just in terms of capacities, such as power or lifespan, but in kind. Only an indirect relationship with divinity is possible (which, as we have seen, the Maggid argues as well). While philosophy arrogantly tries to use reason and reduce religious matters into clear, reliable, and accessible forms of knowledge, Kierkegaard writes that genuine religion is irreducible— it is "not a doctrine, but an existential contradiction." It is not sufficient for a spiritual person to philosophize about the categories of faith, concepts such as God, the soul, sin, and suffering. One must *inhabit* them—along with the discomfort and tension that they will inevitably engender in us.

The radical gulf of difference between humanity and God is most obvious in the arena of rationality. Kierkegaard urges us to withdraw our confidence in and reliance on the faculty of reason, for it will never be capable of a direct apprehension of the divine, of grasping what is fundamentally different from itself; human reason not only has limits and restraints, it *should* be restrained. For him, the great paradox of rational thought is that it wants "to discover something that thought itself cannot think." The unknown (and unknowable) reality that reason confronts as it strives for insight is none other than God. It may not be accessible, but it exists. Our relationship with this Mystery transcends our conceptualization of it. Kierkegaard's God (like the Kotzker Rebbe's, as we discussed in the preceding chapter) is "hidden." When we try to define God, we treat God as an object, a thing, and we interfere with and distance ourselves from our dynamic with the divine. That is when restraint can function as a mechanism for potentially revelatory moments.

Since it is linked to the conflict between the believer's boundless passion for "truth" and the immovable wall of uncertainty, authentic faith involves a strong element of risk. In this respect, faith starts where thought ends. Because the goal of the believer is an impenetrable paradox, faith is, for Kierkegaard, an offense to the mind, a painful affront to our profound craving for intellectual comprehension. Faith must be an act of the *will*, the result not of rational argumentation, but of an existential leap toward the unknown. Yet faith is not and cannot be a permanent state, a sustained, comfortable place of rest. It is a constant and sometimes harrowing struggle, a fight, the ultimate state of tension. Faith must be renewed perpetually, again and again, like the repetitive behavior of the figures who leap up for heaven in the Kotzker's parable on the human condition.

That is why only a warrior, or a "knight," is able to face this ordeal. It takes wisdom and power to contract and constrain power, to reside in a realm of ambiguity.

I highlighted both Abraham and the Akedah story in the previous chapter. Kierkegaard has much to say about both subjects, most famously in his masterwork, *Fear and Trembling*. For him, Abraham is the very quintessence of the spiritual warrior, his knight of faith. Kierkegaard writes of the patriarch: "He knew it was God the Almighty who was testing him; he knew it was the hardest sacrifice that could be demanded of him; but he knew also that no sacrifice is too severe when God demands it—and he drew the knife."

Kierkegaard goes on to explain why Abraham is the model of how we, too, must confront the trials and challenges in our lives, no matter how intense, overwhelming, or absurd the situation might be:

> If Abraham had doubted as he stood there on Mount Moriah, if irresolute he had looked around, if he had happened to spot the ram before drawing the knife, if God had allowed him to sacrifice it instead of Isaac—then he would have gone home, everything would have been the same . . . his return would have been a flight, his deliverance an accident, his reward disgrace, his future perhaps perdition. Then he would have witnessed neither to his faith nor to God's grace. . . . Venerable Father Abraham! When you went home from Mount Moriah, you did not need a eulogy to comfort you for what was lost, for you gained everything and kept Isaac—was it not so?

The power that inheres in Abraham is directly related to his ability to restrain and subordinate his will to the will of God. In the same paradoxical act of attempting to sacrifice Isaac, Abraham believes, though absurdly, that he will get his beloved son back. The patriarch acts with radical resignation in that he is prepared to give up the very thing he most wants to keep. And yet, simultaneously, Abraham possesses the faith that Isaac will be spared. While relinquishing hope, he nevertheless expects the impossible.

The knight of faith can stare straight into the abyss, into the face of the impossible, and believe nonetheless. That hallmark capacity—the strength to embrace absurdity and paradox—has given Kierkegaard's vision of the spiritual warrior some resonance in areas of our own popular culture. Some have compared the knight of faith to the Jedi masters in the *Star Wars* film series, or to the enigmatic character Morpheus in the *Matrix* trilogy. Yet despite the dramatic nature of such a figure, all the knight's activity occurs internally, unseen by the outside world. Kierkegaard writes that "if one did not know him, it would be impossible to distinguish him from the rest of the crowd."

What truly matters on the spiritual journey is not what we do, but who we are. Even the most meek and modest human being possesses the potential to evolve into a warrior of the spirit. What follows is one of Kierkegaard's most poignant descriptions of the knight of faith, a passage that also conveys the loneliness that position can entail:

This man has made and at every moment is making the movement of infinity. . . . He resigned everything infinitely, and then he grasped everything again by virtue of the absurd. . . . Most people live completely absorbed in worldly joys and sorrows; they are benchwarmers who do not take part in the dance. The knights of infinity are ballet dancers and have elevation. They make the upward movement and come down again. But every time they come down, they are unable to assume the posture immediately, they waver for a moment, and this wavering shows that they are aliens in the world. It is more or less conspicuous according to their skill, but even the most skillful of these knights cannot hide this wavering. . . . To be able to come down in such a way that instantaneously one seems to stand and to walk, to change the leap into life into walking, absolutely to express the sublime in the pedestrian—only that knight can do it, and this is the one and only marvel.

Kierkegaard's knight dwells in a metaphysical dance, "wavering" in a place of ambiguity and mystery that most of us could not tolerate. Yet this capacity to waver, to exist between two worlds, so to speak, is what gives the knight his or her great spiritual power and the ability to uncover—and express—the holiness that is too often hidden from us in our everyday lives. Only the knight of faith can see God everywhere and in all things—including in adversity and pain. That is the marvel of such a person. That is the gift.

THE STRENGTH OF SUBTLETY

This chapter has concentrated on the idea that oftentimes we must engage with our obstacles—and sometimes even with ourselves—in indirect and subtle ways, ways that involve restraint, tolerance, patience, compassion, and humility. That is how we season and strengthen our souls. Kierkegaard's knight is an ideal, a challenge, and an abstract goal. Our task as mere mortals is to identify, nourish, and develop the best that is within each of us—and then strive with all of our might to become spiritual warriors. The outcome will be different for each person, but that is precisely the point. As he neared his death, Rabbi Zusya came to realize that his life's work was never to be like the great Moses, but to be the very best Zusya he could possibly be. Our charge is the same.

Engagement, whether in a fight situation or in our relationship with our souls, to others, or to God, takes many forms, and it is usually the particular context that will determine how we ought to act. We have explored what several religious thinkers and mystics have said about spiritual engagement, human behavior, and the role of indirect contact. Some martial arts systems (such as aikido and judo) do not even possess direct, frontal strikes as part of their method of engagement. I have learned over the years that, when facing interpersonal challenges, two well-known sports clichés are fundamentally accurate in their insights and applications: first, that the best offense is often a strong and effective defense; and second, that in certain situations, the most successful path to victory over opponents in a contest is to use their own force or energy against them.

How does all of this relate to our program of self-empowerment? Yet again, what seems paradoxical at the surface actually masks a deeper truth. In the context of personal growth (as well as in the workplace), this reality has some extremely useful and practical applications that flow from it—and I have experienced a number of them firsthand.

From the perspective of a rabbi, a synagogue—or any kind of congregation, for that matter—can sometimes seem like a veritable petri dish of interpersonal conflicts, a place where people vie for power, project their problems, play out their issues, and lay out their baggage (sometimes dating as far back as adolescence or childhood). Dealing with complex psychological needs and diverse emotional dispositions often consumes more of my time and effort than does the cultivation of meaningful spirituality, let alone the transmission of Judaism and Jewish practice to the members of my community.

Many people today say that timing is everything. Centuries ago, the Jewish sage Kohelet said: "There is a season for everything, a time for every experience under heaven" (Ecclesiastes 3:1). I think there is great wisdom in that observation. But knowing when to act, and in what way, is often a challenge for most of us. In my own congregational work, I have faced serious financial dilemmas, membership concerns, disagreements and tensions with other staff members and lay leaders, and countless other issues that called for me to respond. I have also dealt with some very difficult, and at times troubled, personalities both inside and outside of the communities I have served.

Timing *is* everything—not in and of itself, but as it relates to specific situations and contexts. You certainly don't have to belong to the clergy in order to be a spiritual warrior, but you do have to work hard at developing the inner capabilities and skills that we have discussed throughout this book. Indirect engagement is one of them. We might possess souls that are open, bold, creative, and resolute, yet despite the fact that each of those capacities is a vital component in the life and work of a spiritual warrior, they are not always the appropriate ones to tap in to in every potential scenario. We need to know when to hold back, when to step aside, and also when to let go. This is where experience and intuition play such critically important roles in our decision making and in our actions, and where we get to witness who the true masters of the spirit really are.

Different kinds of conflicts require different kinds of strategies and sets of tactics. To me, this is as valid a principle for a congregation as it is on the battlefield or in a stadium. When it comes to human interactions, atmosphere should inform our attitude and reaction should influence our response. I always attempt to take both into account.

I recall one congregant vividly, a rather saturnine man who would always give me a hard time during the discussion part of our worship services. He would challenge me on virtually every topic I ever spoke about, and he'd become especially agitated and confrontational when it came to subjects that had to do with God. I didn't mind our exchanges, but others began to complain to me about his sometimes aggressive attitude and behavior, and when his presence and actions reached the point that I felt he was starting to discomfort and alienate members of our community and interfere with their own experiences, I invited him to sit down and meet with me, face-to-face, as his rabbi. To my great pleasure, he accepted. This was an opportunity for me to grow as a pastor and to try to help him grow as a thoughtful, seeking, struggling human being.

I knew that the environment of our meeting had the potential to become tense and divisive, so I braced myself and adopted an attitude of serenity (in order to defuse any emotionalism) and a strategy of indirection (so as to minimize any combativeness). We were on the same team, after all, and my ultimate goal was to offer words that would make this congregant feel more at ease with his community, his faith, and his own soul.

We met in my office. I pulled my chair to the front of my desk, next to his, and we sat directly across from each other. The man declined my offer of a soda or some coffee, so I decided to cut to the chase and ask him a question: "What's up, my friend?"

He knew what I was getting at. "I just don't believe in God," he answered. "Not at all. I come to services out of respect for the memory of my parents. I pay my dues on time, and I send my kids to religious school, but I think this whole thing is one big lie."

"I get it," I replied. And then I tried to transform the situation by redirecting my next question so that the tables were now turned on him: "When you say the word *God*, though, which particular concept of God is it that you reject with so much vehemence?"

I wasn't trying to avoid his concerns—I was simply allowing him to let the force of his own energy and aggression lead us toward a greater good. "What do you mean?"

"I mean," I said, "there are many conceptions and images of God in Judaism, especially in the Bible. Dozens, even more. A lot of them actually contradict one another. So I may very well share your disbelief in whatever idea of God it is that you possess."

We spent the next hour discussing, very calmly, the many and varied ideas about God in the Jewish tradition. The man was interested and intrigued; he had no idea that there were so many different views of who, or what, constituted the Transcendent.

"Maybe it's not that you don't believe in God," I suggested. "Maybe it's that you haven't yet been exposed to a concept of God you can resonate with. Think about it."

I was playing a kind of "verbal judo" with the man, but I meant every word that I said. He would never have responded in a positive way had I been defensive, apologetic, didactic, or confrontational. By approaching his questions and struggles indirectly, by framing our dialogue in a nonpolemical, noncombative fashion (so that there were no absolutes, no rigid "right" and "wrong" answers), we'd begun a relationship, and I had pried open his mind—at least to ponder the possibility that there *might* be a "God" who is far more sophisticated and worthy of serious discussion than the pediatric conceptions and images too many of us still hold. This man eventually became a regular participant in my adult education classes, and he taught me that, more often than not, an effective spiritual leader needs to be sensitive and subtle, especially in his or her capacity as a pastor—even if someone in the congregation is acting in ways that seem problematic.

Indirect engagement can be applied as a technique not just for handling conflicts, but for achieving success and uplift in other arenas of human dynamics and relations.

In the boxing ring, a successful fighter will often avoid an opponent's punches through bobbing and weaving, rather than trying to block them in a frontal, linear way. This tactic allows the boxer to absorb less punishment and conserve more energy, and it usually results in a victory. In the setting of a sanctuary, my task as a rabbi is not to evade, but to *evoke*—emotions, thoughts, memories. My opponents are the petty but numerous distractions of modern life, and my weapons are my words. When I preach, I strive for evocation, not indoctrination, in the hearts and souls of my congregants. I use my sermons to invite dialogue, not to instill dogma. And I have found this tactic to be extremely helpful as a subtle, indirect way of inspiring and empowering those who need my support and guidance. In my world, a "knockout" occurs when I am able to draw out the best, most sacred elements within the men and women under my watch.

As we saw through the examples of tzimtzum, that will sometimes mean I have to take a step back, or a step to the side, in order to create the space for someone I might be working with to mature and evolve into a better person and/or Jew. At other times, such as when I am engaged with a person who is in a place where I simply *cannot* reach them (either as a result of their own issues, or owing to the fact that we are just a poor combination), I have to know when to let go. The bottom line, and the challenge, is that the spiritual warrior needs to strive—with thought and vigor—to find the proper balance in all of his or her interactions and relationships, particularly with his or her own soul.

8

A JOURNEY THAT NEVER ENDS

THE POET T. S. ELIOT writes, "What we call the beginning is often the end / And to make an end is to make a beginning." The path of the spiritual warrior is a path that never comes to a close with rigid, black-and-white finality. It is the ongoing human journey itself, filled with twists and turns, fits and starts, closures to old chapters and openings to new ones. It is a journey that can involve great struggle, yet the battle-tested warrior knows how to embrace that struggle, mature from it, and ultimately persevere.

As we have discussed, stamina, as a key component in our program of self-empowerment, relates to our capacity to endure adversity, to persist. Perseverance does more. This final quality relates to our ability to *advance,* to view adversity in a more philosophical light, as an opportunity for growth. We will always encounter new challenges and obstacles that we must endure; the virtue of perseverance ought not be conceived of as one long race, but as a series of countless short races, one after the other. We will not and cannot win all of them, but, in the words of William James, "Most people never run far enough on their first wind to find out they've got a second." The mission of the spiritual warrior is to strive—in perpetuity—to gain and regain our second wind, to have the foresight to see past our losses and the strength to push beyond them.

When I finally earned my black belt in karate, I did not become a martial arts master, and when I was ordained as a rabbi, I was not suddenly transformed into a religious sage. I had no "And thus it ends!" moment. Both of these hard-won experiences were just the beginning of deeper, increasingly challenging adventures that would come.

The same could be said for the others whose harrowing personal stories I have interwoven with the teachings of sages, mystics, biblical figures, and other thinkers throughout this book. We have seen people endure, and grow from, their experiences with despair, fear, rage, anxiety, guilt, self-doubt, and other difficult emotions. Yet even after making it through their particular dark nights of the soul, none of the people I interviewed looked back at the events that caused such discomforting feelings as having had concrete endings. Instead, they viewed them as learning opportunities that helped them to start afresh. They saw the process itself, and the tools it provided them with to venture forth on their journeys, as the most important aspect of their narratives.

THE VALUE OF SEMICOLONS

It is only if we learn to accept the reality that the road of a warrior is one without an end—and that we are bound to encounter struggles and paradoxes while on our journeys—that we can move forward. This is no easy task, and it has vexed our fellow travelers for millennia. The book of Ecclesiastes opens with its world-weary author, Kohelet, expressing perplexity (and even a sense of indignation) at one of life's such apparent paradoxes—the fact that sinner and saint, fool and sage, poor and rich all share the same ultimate fate. "How can the wise man die like the fool?" Kohelet inquires, recounting the reflections of his younger, but no less curious years. "And so I hated life, because all the work done beneath the sun seemed worthless to me; for all is vanity and a striving after wind" (Ecclesiastes 2:16–17). Why work hard when nothing really matters in the end?

With the passage of time and a more evolved perspective, Kohelet is eventually able to move beyond his earlier fear and loathing. By the conclusion of the book, he seems more at ease not just with his questions about mortality, but with the never-ending contradictions inherent in the human condition. "Of making many books there is no end," Kohelet states, "and much study is a weariness of the flesh" (Ecclesiastes 12:12). Our finite knowledge is not sufficient to penetrate the mysteries of the universe. Acceptance of uncertainty is a much healthier strategy for living than is our futile resistance to it.

As I will note with subsequent biblical examples from my book *Craving the Divine,* there are times when we move not only from one attitude to another but from one place to another. Shortly after their flight from Egypt, the people of Israel find themselves trapped against the shore of the Reed Sea by Pharaoh's army, and they begin to panic. In front of them is a seemingly impassable body of water, and behind them are vengeful and fast-moving Egyptian troops and charioteers. Their terror, as well as their uncertainty (and near-paralysis) about what to do, is understandable. God directs Moses to order them to "journey forward" (Exodus 14:15). It is only when the Israelites take that first step, when they make a resolute leap into the unknown, that God intervenes in the grave situation.

At that moment, a miracle transpires, one known to a great many of us: "Moses held out his arm over the sea and the Lord drove back the sea with a strong east wind all that night, and turned the sea into dry ground. The waters were split, and the Israelites went into the sea on dry ground, the waters forming a wall for them on their right and on their left" (Exodus 14:21–22). God helps the Israelites further by confusing the minds of the Egyptians—in hot pursuit of their former slaves across the floor of the sea—who start to panic and eventually try to retreat. Once the people of Israel emerge onto solid ground, the waters of the sea collapse, falling back to their natural position and drowning all of Pharaoh's troops.

Rabbi Simcha Bunim of Peshischa (1765–1827), an early Hasidic mystic, has an interesting interpretation of this (in)famous event. For him, the splitting of the Reed Sea is significant not because of its historicity, but because it teaches us a profound lesson about what it means to be human and to confront adversity. Simcha Bunim understands the episode as an expression of a deep and metaphorical inner transformation. He suggests that the parting of the Reed Sea represents a phenomenon of radical liberation in the lives of the Israelites, the moment in which they finally overcome their fear of the Egyptians, a fear they had lived with for centuries. What the Torah seems to relate as an event that occurs "out there" should be read instead as an allusion to something that takes place *within,* a metamorphosis inside the hearts and souls of the people of Israel.

What immediately follows Israel's passage from fear to hope, from struggle to survival, from death to new life, is a song—a joyous, communal expression of victory and thanksgiving. When this Song at the Sea is read or chanted aloud in a synagogue, it is customary for all those who are present to stand until its completion. The only other scriptural passage that is bestowed this sign of special respect is that of the Ten Commandments. This song lauds God's might and majesty, and it conveys the Israelites' gratitude for everything the divine Creator has done for them during their many ordeals:

> I will sing to the Lord, for he is highly exalted;
> Horse and driver he has hurled into the sea.
> The Lord is my strength and song;
> He is become my salvation;
> This is my God and I will enshrine him;
> The God of my father, and I will exalt him. . . .

> Who is like you, O Lord, among the celestials;
> Who is like you, majestic in holiness,
> Awesome in splendor, working wonders? (Exodus 15:1–2, 11)

This ancient song of praise also highlights Israel's unfolding and evolving desert pilgrimage, its transition from one stage in its sacred journey to the next. After describing the adversaries who still threaten Israel's destiny, the song goes on:

> Terror and dread descend upon them;
> Through the might of your arm they are still as stone—
> Till your people cross over, O Lord,
> Till your people cross over whom you have ransomed.
> You will bring them and plant them in your own mountain,
> The place you made to dwell in, O Lord,
> The sanctuary, O Lord, which your hands established.
> The Lord will reign forever and ever! (Exodus 15:16–18)

Some psychologists and other thinkers view biblical images of water and land as representations of internal states. In Psalm 69, during a trial in his life, water becomes a metaphor for David's sense that he is drowning ("this flood overwhelms me") in an existential struggle; in the book of Jonah, the reluctant prophet is expelled onto land by a giant fish after he has wrestled with his own demons and essentially been "baptized" under the sea. The tough path of the Israelites from the Reed Sea, to dry land, to Mount Sinai is a similar journey from crisis to emergence, from troubled start to ongoing trek.

When the collective Song at the Sea concludes, the prophetess Miriam takes a timbrel in her hand and, with the other women and their instruments, leads an ecstatic dance and a chant of rejoicing. This spontaneous act of celebration is their response to the physical and emotional shift that has just occurred in their community and their lives. It underscores a profound awareness that—with divine aid—they have faced adversity and peril and ultimately persevered through the experience, not only intact, but triumphant.

A person who recites the Song at the Sea "audibly and joyfully" (Miriam sings a refrain from the song in Exodus 15:21) is, according to one mystical tradition, immediately pardoned for his or her sins and transgressions. What does this teaching imply? All we really need to achieve inner redemption is to appreciate and affirm our lives—and to acknowledge God's presence and role in them. Miriam's demonstration of how to behave when we have made it through an arduous journey should be a model for us today, in this troubled era when such public expressions of joy and gratitude are rare.

Nevertheless, rapturous joy is not and cannot be a constant, uninterrupted human state. Miriam's journey, like all of our journeys, continues. The Israelites, in the very next verse, find themselves thirsty and anxious in the wilderness of Shur. Their struggle to reach the Promised Land is not over—they will wander for years to come. The people of Israel will get lost, they will get hungry, they will lose patience, they will rebel, but then they will gain their "second wind" and move forward once more. Their relentless march through the vast desert is a paradigm for the way warriors of the spirit, following Miriam's lead, should pursue (and perceive) their own lives. For human life is punctuated by semicolons, not periods; it is a staggered, ongoing, difficult process of fits and starts.

ETERNAL STRIVING

The human journey can be beautiful, but it is also fraught with recurring dangers that lurk along the way. As the Torah warns us from its earliest verses, "Sin crouches at the door; its urge is toward you" (Genesis 4:7). For a spiritual warrior, a person who has devoted his or her life to the process of inner development and advancement, that sin, that enemy, is self-satisfaction. As we achieve ever higher levels of spiritual empowerment, and as the various and interconnected parts of our souls (NaRaN, or nefesh, ruach, and neshamah) continue to grow and evolve, new obstacles will inevitably arise—and complacency is among the most dangerous of them. For complacency puts into jeopardy our fundamental mission, the striving for ego-transcendence and the drive to protect and perfect our world. That's the warrior's challenge and charge, and it is a ceaseless one.

One of the most compelling and misunderstood of history's spiritual warriors, a philosopher who grasped very clearly the idea of striving as a ceaseless, lifelong activity, was Friedrich Nietzsche (1844–1900), whom we noted briefly in chapter 4 in our discussion of courage. As was the case with Kierkegaard, Nietzsche's father was a devoutly religious man—in this case, though, he was also a pastor with his own parish, in the tiny Prussian village of Röcken, near Leipzig. His father died when Friedrich was only four years old, and the trauma of the event left a deep impression on Nietzsche's soul and worldview. The family soon moved to the larger city of Naumburg, and from that point forward the young Nietzsche began his studies and his exposure to the wider cultural and intellectual world. He was an intense, serious student, and as a child he was referred to as "the little pastor." This would prove to be an ironic title as he grew older.

Nietzsche would ultimately turn his back on organized religion (and on Christianity, specifically). Yet he would develop a profound, though highly unconventional, sort of spirituality— one that was daring, innovative, and unique, a spirituality that had more core elements in common with many of the other warriors whom we have explored in this book than might be apparent to the reader at first blush.

Central to Nietzsche's philosophical system is the quality of perseverance, or what he calls the "myth of eternal return." For Nietzsche, cultivating the capacity to confront life's unrelenting, unending struggles not just with quiet serenity but with joy is itself an act of courage. The first requirement of intellectual honesty is to accept the human condition exactly as it is, to the exclusion of any want, yearning, or aspiration beyond it, with all its drives and dark impulses, as well as with the spiritual powers of humanity's intellect and creativity. The focus of all these forces is on the endless attempt to "complete" themselves—not in a straight line of progressive evolution, but in perpetually recurring cycles of effort through which, at times, an Overman (*Übermensch*) will emerge—a surpassing human being of superior integrity, bravery, and creative will whom each cycle of life seeks as the hope toward its fulfillment. For the Overman, eternal striving is itself eternally enough, despite the fact that this striving never ends.

Nietzsche expresses this idea in his work *The Eternal Return:*

> Your whole life will always be turned over like an hourglass and will run out again and again—with one great moment in between, until all conditions from which you arose, will come together again in the cyclic motion of the world. And then you will find again every pain, every joy, every friend and enemy, and every hope and error, and every blade of grass and ray of light, the whole interrelationship of all things. This ring, of which you are a particle, will shine forth again and again. And in every cycle of human life there is always an hour when first to one, then to many, then to all the mightiest idea appears: that of eternal recurrence. . . . The task is to live so that you must *wish* to live again.

The great inspiration for this conception of life was the Hellenistic myth of Dionysus, who is eternally dismembered and destroyed but, paradoxically, recurrently reconstituted and reborn. For Nietzsche, the will of Dionysus for regeneration, rebirth, and renewal foreshadows the Overman's will to power, to the fullness of his own potentialities. It is not a power over others, but the realization of all that is dormant and divine within *himself:* life constantly transfiguring itself in eternally recurring cycles, each of immeasurable duration, and yet, as a whole, eternally remaining itself. The Overman is the literal embodiment of the life force—evolving, dynamic, ungraspable, never satisfied with himself or his successes, forever in a state of becoming.

Similar to Kierkegaard's knight of faith, Nietzsche's Overman is a vision, a messianic ideal, a goal that the spiritual warrior must strive for, always.

The mythic manifestation of the Overman can be found most clearly through the figure of Zarathustra in Nietzche's famous book, *Thus Spoke Zarathustra*. This collection of aphorisms, images, and parables uses the prophetic and poetic Zarathustra to point the way (but only for the most valiant and free-spirited among us) toward the Overman. "Where is the lightning which might lick you with its tongue?" asks Zarathustra. "Where is the madness with which you should have been inoculated? Behold, I teach you the Overman. He is this lightning; he is this madness."

Whether because of its mythic nature, its poetic appeal, or the sheer attraction of Nietzsche's bold cry to the world to affirm life at its most primal, powerful level, this strange literary work has been misread, abused, and manipulated over the years in unfortunate and, in a few notorious cases (e.g., with Hitler and his Nazi theoreticians), horrific ways. I want to reclaim it as a manifesto on the majesty of being human—because it warrants a place among the works and figures we've discussed.

At one point in the book, Zarathustra—adventurer, experimenter, and seeker that he is—embarks on a sea voyage to find a new and undiscovered island. During the voyage, Zarathustra relates a vision to his fellow seafarers, one that haunts him yet offers a hint of what he hopes to find when he reaches land and begins his exploration:

> I walked gloomily through the colorless twilight, gloomy and hard, with compressed lips. More than one sun had set. A path which rose defiantly through the rolling stones, a malicious, lonely path, friendly to neither weeds nor bush, a mountain path crunched under the defiance of my foot. Walking along silently over the mocking tinkling of the pebbles and crunching the stone that would have me slip, I forced my feet upwards. Upwards—in defiance of the spirit

that would drag me down into the abyss, the spirit of gravity, my devil and archenemy. Upwards, though this spirit sat upon me, half dwarf, half mole; lame himself and making me lame; dripping lead into my ears and thoughts like drops of lead into my brain! . . . I climbed and climbed, I dreamed and thought, but everything oppressed me. I was like a sick person whom severe torture has exhausted, and, then, a worse dream has awakened. But there is something in me that I call courage; that has hitherto slain every discouragement. This courage finally bade me to stand still and say: "Dwarf! You or I!" . . . Courage is the best slayer, courage that attacks. It slays even death, for it says: "Was *that* life? Very well! Once again!"

Zarathustra views gravity, the force that fights him as he strives to ascend the mountain, as his "devil and archenemy." For Nietzsche, gravity represents *any* force that holds down the human spirit. Yet rather than accepting this encumbrance, Zarathustra throws it off through the pronouncement of the dangerously daring idea of the eternal return. He seems to be spitting in the face of all that would hinder his advance; he seems to be saying, *Is that all you can do to try to stop me? Fine. Let's do this all over again!*

To accept life in its entirety—and to see it forever return in cycles—means to know it in all its details, to understand how weaknesses outnumber strengths, to grasp what an infinite task our own transcendence must become at this realization. Further, transcendence is itself merely the recurrent effort of those few individuals within each cycle who are strong enough to face the reality of the return boldly, despite the enormity of the task. These figures embrace finitude even as they defy it; they affirm life even as it thwarts them at every turn. Yet because they have reached the heights most of us will never see, they are able "to say no like the storm, and to say yes like the clear sky says yes." The Overman will return eternally to give evidence of the dignity of humanity, a conception more severe but also more complete, an idea rooted in endless perseverance.

We ordinary human beings, including those of us who strive to become warriors of the spirit, are existential bridges to the Overman: "Man is a rope," says Zarathustra, "tied between beast and Overman—a rope over an abyss. A dangerous going over, a dangerous on-the-way, a dangerous looking back, a dangerous shudder and a standing still. What is great about man is that he is a bridge, and not a goal; what can be loved in man is that he is a *going over* and a *going under*." If the spirituality of the Overman is anchored in the robust affirmation of his own humanity, and if this is our ideal, then the denial of our humanity is the "abyss" that is, and will ever be, waiting beneath our feet.

For Nietzsche, humanity is the embodiment of the paradox of "going over" and "going under." What his stand-in, Zarathustra, loves in us most is our capability to live as tightrope walkers, neither at beginnings nor at ends, but always at both; he has faith in our boundless potential, but simultaneously recognizes that we are bound by the constrictions of our very humanity. This image bears some striking similarities to the "leaping" figures in the Kotzker Rebbe's parable and the "wavering" of Kierkegaard's knights of faith. What is their message? It is dangerous to be human. Our fears, fantasies, delusions, and denials can injure our evolving souls. Zarathustra sees man as a bridge, as a perpetual *becoming*, not as a finished product. Humanity's only mission in this life is to persevere, and, for Nietzsche (as opposed to most of the other thinkers we have discussed), "God" does not have to enter into the picture for that to occur. The Overman represents the fulfillment of this cyclic journey, where he finds his self-transcendence through his own self-actualization—which is the joyful embrace of the realization of his eternal return.

In a section of *Thus Spoke Zarathustra* called "On War and Warriors," Nietzsche seems to speak directly to us, to the reality of the difficulties of the path of the spiritual warrior, who can

only find his or her fulfillment through the idealized and messianic conception of the Overman:

> If you cannot be saints of knowledge, then at least be its
> warriors. They are companions and forerunners of such
> saintliness. I see many soldiers; would that I saw many
> warriors! "Uniform," they call what they wear. I hope that
> it is not uniformity that they hide with it! You should be
> one whose eyes always are looking for an enemy—*your*
> enemy. . . . To a good warrior, "thou shalt" is more pleas-
> ant than "I will." Every thing that you love must first have
> been given to you as a command. Let your love of life be
> love of your highest hope; and your highest hope should
> be the highest idea of life! But you must permit your high-
> est thought to be commanded by me—and it reads: man
> is something that must be overcome. Thus live your life of
> obedience and war! What is there to a long life? What war-
> rior wishes to be spared! I am not sparing you; I love you
> wholly, my brothers in war! Thus spoke Zarathustra.

In this passage, we have an expression of the charge that we,
as spiritual warriors, must hearken to if we are to "overcome" the
obstacles that prevent us from embracing the idea of eternal re-
currence. There will be many adversaries in our path as we strive
toward the vision of the Overman, and we must be prepared for
a lifetime of battle and struggle. Most of the fundamental principles in our own program of growth—vigilance, humility, creativity, discipline, courage—are present here, and they will come
into play as we each confront our individual enemies. For Nietzsche, the warrior will find his or her greatest nobility not through
the illusion of freedom but through submission and sacrifice—
to dreams, to hopes, to the love of life itself. The purpose of our
lives resides not in their duration, but in their quality. Striving
boldly through life, facing its recurrent cycles with fortitude,
dignity, and honor, is our most formidable ordeal, yet also our
highest reward.

BEYOND GROUND ZERO

F. Scott Fitzgerald writes that "vitality shows in not only the ability to persist but the ability to start over." In this chapter, we have discussed the importance of regaining our second wind even when we are exhausted, we have explored the mythic idea of eternal return, and we have observed the repetitive and often staggered nature that is so much a part of the human journey. In the world of art, creation is usually a one-time act: once produced and completed, you can leave behind a painting, a sculpture, or a book. That is why we have museums and libraries. Yet in the arena of our complicated, all-too-human lives, creation and re-creation go hand in hand in a ceaseless, ongoing way— beginnings and endings are intertwined. We express our "vitality" when we advance, particularly if that advance follows a failure or a disappointment, or even a tragedy.

About a week after the collapse of the World Trade Center on September 11, 2001, I walked through Ground Zero. It was during the Days of Awe. Before me was a scene of apocalyptic devastation: a wasteland of smashed buildings and shattered windows; hideous pillars of twisted steel; plumes of smoke rising eerily from the rubble.

As a law enforcement chaplain, I talked to cops, agents, firefighters, and rescue workers from dozens of agencies and cities. I remember one K-9 unit, a sheriff's deputy and his dog. Even though by that point all they were pulling out were bodies, his Labrador retriever wouldn't let him sleep. Everyone there, whether human or animal, was focused on their work, on trying to serve in whatever capacity they could.

I was moved by the acts of commitment and expressions of love that permeated that hellish place. And I was astounded by the vision of so many people finding their deepest, most beautiful selves in the heart of such an immense void. There was a sense of community—and a spirituality—present there that I have not witnessed before or since. I saw men in various uniforms hugging one another; grizzled hardhats behind bulldozers and in crane cabs openly sobbing; dedicated and exhausted volunteers handing out sandwiches and bottles of water as if they were sacramental objects.

That experience was mirrored when my congregation, The New Shul, held our Rosh Hashanah services only a few blocks north of the terrorist attack, in a church in Greenwich Village. Several of our households had suddenly become homeless and were living out of luggage. Our children were stunned and scared, many having seen with their own eyes men and women leaping to their deaths onto the dust-caked streets in front of them. Our adult members clung to their cell phones tightly, like guardrails, waiting anxiously for news about missing friends, colleagues, and family members. I'd torn up my planned sermons days before. What we did instead was share our collective feelings and thoughts. People spoke, embraced one another, and wept.

Yet no one was alone. We were all on the same journey.

As downtown Manhattan's youngest synagogue, we had been in existence at that point for only a couple of years, but the fact that we'd created a community—and a *sanctuary*, a true safe haven in the best sense of the word—for those who now so desperately craved one was as palpable as it was profound. I felt a sense of intense pride in what we had accomplished in such a relatively brief period of time.

After the horrors of 9/11, lower Manhattan began to undergo great change, development, and rebirth—and that applied to the Jewish community, too. Those who had been made homeless by homicidal Islamic extremists gradually began to return to their damaged homes. As new high-rise residential buildings started to go up, Jews from around the city began to move down from other areas. With more Jews now in need of more Jewish activities and communities, there was a slow but steady increase in Jewish life and institutions below 14th Street, and a vitality and dynamism that I'd rarely seen in my years of working as a New York City rabbi.

In close parallel with our own philosophy when we founded The New Shul pre-9/11, most of these *post*-9/11 initiatives strived to reflect both the creativity and the sensibility of the Jews who were attracted to these neighborhoods.

High-profile Jewish arts and culture festivals started drawing large crowds and taking place in unusual venues; a group called Tribeca Hebrew created a new religious school that held its classes in the basement of a storefront; the Soho Synagogue, a Chabad-led congregation, threw lavish Kabbalat Shabbat cocktail parties; the 14th Street Y, under the auspices of the venerable Educational Alliance, worked to reinvent itself as an outpost of East Village hipness; the Downtown Kehillah, a multidenominational consortium of downtown synagogues, tried to build bridges between communities; and the Jewish Community Project, a self-styled "alternative" version of the old and established 92nd Street Y, emerged out of this same impulse and energy.

Downtown Jewish life has started over, and it has persevered, even thrived. So has life in lower Manhattan more generally. It has been a triumph over tragedy. Bold, determined, and risk-taking spiritual warriors have begun to come out of the woodwork of one of America's most cynical and jaded cities. Men and women who hadn't cared much about spirituality or self-transcendence suddenly, in the shadow of fear and trauma, have opened up and reached beyond themselves. It is a wonder to behold.

Most of these initiatives share certain traits, characteristics that we had already lined into the fabric of our own community years before: a "come as you are" attitude with a focus on inclusivity for all, regardless of belief or background; a grassroots, egalitarian approach to religious life; a decentralized leadership structure; a tendency toward non- or post-denominational Judaism; multiple and diverse paths for expressing one's Jewish identity; an eclecticism in vision and in mission. And I see similar trends in congregations of other faiths—along with the same vibrancy and vitality.

At the core of all of this, of course, was a widespread disaffection with, and a detachment from, the previous status quo. Why else build something new?

Yet these new institutions and initiatives have made some of the founding members of my community (and, to be frank, myself) feel a bit like seasoned pioneers—a very strange sensation for a young congregation like ours. But they have also made us feel that we are not alone in craving a new kind of spiritual community, one that is more reflective of the kind of people we actually are—and that we'd like to be.

Nearly a decade has now passed. And with the shift in downtown demographics has come a concurrent and marked shift in mindset. This has also meant that new problems have gradually but inexorably emerged—as they always do whenever we reach those fluid points of intersection between ends and beginnings. As a rabbi who has been able to bear witness to the changes in and renewal of Jewish life in lower Manhattan both before and after 9/11, I have the privilege of a unique and firsthand perspective on attitudes and their real-world results. Working here in the trenches, I have to say that I do not like everything that I have seen.

Although commitment is a basic and essential quality of the spiritual warrior, *committed* is not a word I would use to describe the typical downtown Jew in this post-9/11 world. Speaking for my peers, we want some form of Jewish life, but we want it on our own terms, at times when it is convenient for us, and in small, easy-to-swallow doses. We do not want a lot of expectations placed on us. We want to be entertained, not challenged. We want, as one person once put it to me, "just the fun stuff," without any of the communal responsibility our faith associates with being a member of the Jewish people. We're not into the serious exploration of Jewish texts and practices, but we (and our leaders) are preoccupied with, almost obsessed by, the idea of "edginess." Moreover, our new efforts are beginning to fall prey to age-old problems: territorialism, politics, redundancy, a lack of heartfelt unity.

As someone who has served downtown Jews for ten years, it is clear to me that we must remain as vigilant as ever today, but in radically new ways. Anti-Semitism, intermarriage, and assimilation are not my biggest concerns.

My biggest worries are vapidity and self-satisfaction.

When viewed through the lens of history, Jews have always been engaged in the process of recreating Judaism and Jewish life in our own image. That process should continue. But we need to make sure that that image is not only creative and dynamic, but also true to our tradition's roots, those anchors that have made us who we are.

The specter of terrorism is still very much with us, along with its associated fears and anxieties. We must stand our guard and be vigilant—not just from a martial position, but from a psychic standpoint as well. We cannot allow life's darker forces to dictate our efforts or motivate our behavior. We must bear in mind that the dynamic interplay of ends and beginnings will never cease. Our sense of mission must arise from within. We must be proactive, not merely reactive to external events. That will only lead to an inevitable corruption of our work. Our advancement is directly linked to our courage, our capacity to observe the culture around us and, when necessary, shout, "No!"

For the warrior on the spiritual and moral path, that will sometimes mean having to go to battle against certain trends with all our heart, soul, and being. "Change" as an end in itself is just a hollow slogan. Authentic evolution and advancement must be linked to a consciousness of our history and a strong awareness of lessons learned.

DEMONS, DESERTS, AND THE DRIVE TO PROGRESS

There are times when we can enrich and enlarge our souls within the context of a collective, and times when we can empower them as individuals. If we are fortunate, those moments will sometimes intersect. In either case, however, becoming a spiritual warrior is ultimately about the journey, not the destination; it is about the never-ending task of learning from our experiences, working hard, and moving forward as more mature students and seekers. The "Promised Land" is not so much a place as it is a *process,* a portal to a more robust, enlightened, and purposeful life. Yet the Bible itself is filled with many powerful images, myths, characters, and events that will benefit any sojourner.

We have already discussed Miriam and the Exodus narrative in this chapter and their relationship to the process of evolution and growth. Let's now turn our focus to Moses—and to the end of the Torah itself—for even further insight into this dynamic.

It is an act of violence that marks the entry of Moses into the Jewish journey. The very first time we see the future leader and prophet as an adult—in the second chapter of the book of Exodus—he kills a man. While the victim is an abusive Egyptian taskmaster, the killing nonetheless forces Moses to flee, deep into the desert of Midian (as we discussed earlier in this book). Wherever we might think this action belongs on the moral spectrum, many of the rabbinic commentators thought it is what ultimately prevents Moses from entering the Promised Land decades later. Minimally, his behavior shows us a violent anger that is not far below the surface and that will erupt on other occasions.

Even though Moses does not kill again with his own hands, his temper and trouble controlling his violent inclinations express themselves in other, less lethal ways. While Moses communes with God on Mount Sinai, the Israelites, unable or unwilling to wait for his return with the holy covenant, conspire with his brother Aaron, the high priest, to create and worship a statue of a golden calf. Moses catches them in the act:

> As soon as Moses came near the camp and saw the calf and the dancing, he became enraged; and he hurled the tablets from his hands and shattered them at the foot of the mountain. He took the calf that they had made and burnt it; he ground it to powder and strewed it upon the water and so made the Israelites drink it. (Exodus 32:19–20)

The behavior of the people of Israel was terribly misguided. Yet for Moses, their prophet and leader, to willfully demolish the word of God in God's own *presence* seems like a reckless act of sacrilege almost as heinous as the idolatry that so enrages him. This is completely unacceptable. Some of the rabbis try to explain away what Moses does, and claim through a (truly imaginative) midrash that, as Moses approached the camp, the letters of the Ten Commandments detached themselves from the tablets and flew back to God. As a result, the stones grew too heavy for Moses to carry, and he dropped them.

Most rabbis, however, did not absolve the prophet for his grave deed and were willing to acknowledge that he had great difficulty mastering his emotions. Moses was, like each of us, an imperfect human being with problematic sides to his personality. After he destroys the tablets, Moses is not finished—his people must be punished. Moses has the idol melted down and orders the Israelites to drink the gold that they had worshipped as a god just before. His decision, though, seems more the manifestation of a deep anger than an expression of rational deliberation. In addition to this anger, Moses also displays a tendency toward isolation—very possibly a mask for some measure of misanthropy. There are instances in the Torah (such as Exodus 24:18 and 34:3–4) where Moses completely severs contact with the spiritual community that he has been charged with directing and travels alone into the mountains for quite extended periods of time.

To underscore this idea, when Moses does choose to communicate with his people, he demonstrates an authoritarian model of leadership. He doesn't comfort or nurture—he issues decrees and commands, often through intermediaries. Maybe that is why in Exodus 32:1 the Israelites do not to refer to Moses by name, but as "that man."

And yet, despite all of his flaws and shortcomings, Moses belongs solidly among the pantheon of other spiritual warriors we have been highlighting in this book.

Moses is able to mature with age—his personality evolves.

Following many long and arduous years of wandering in the desert, Moses eventually emerges from the trials of the Exodus as a man with genuine understanding, compassion, and love for his people. Close to the conclusion of the book of Deuteronomy (and near the final verses of the Torah, also known as the Five Books of Moses), the prophet gathers together his community and his successor, Joshua, to address them for one of the last times. Moses is now an old man. God has already informed him that he will not be permitted to cross the Jordan with his people. Moses—suppressing whatever feelings of regret, sorrow, or pain he must be experiencing—summons the strength to offer consolation and reassurance:

> The Lord your God himself will cross over at your head; and he will wipe out those nations from your path and you shall dispossess them. . . . Be strong and of good courage, be not in fear or in dread of them; for the Lord your God himself marches with you: He will not fail you or forsake you. (Deuteronomy 31:3, 6)

Although he finally stands at the edge of the Promised Land (aware that even after all of his faith and fortitude, it is a place that he will never enter), Moses focuses not on his own disappointment, but on his divine mission, on the concerns of those he serves.

Moses is prudent, and would not leave the Israelites without a new leader to take his place. He calls Joshua to stand before the whole community and says for all to hear,

> Be strong of good courage, for it is you who shall go with this people into the land that the Lord swore to their fathers to give them, and it is you who shall apportion it to them. And the Lord himself will go before you. He will be with you; he will not fail you or forsake you. Fear not and be not dismayed! (Deuteronomy 31:7–8)

The Moses we see here is not uncaring, angry, or resentful. Far from it. This Moses is a more evolved human being, an individual whose personality has advanced and whose attitude has been transformed by time, experience, and struggle. This inner growth allows Moses to transcend himself, and his words reveal someone capable of a sensitivity—and a serenity of soul—that did not seem possible during his earlier years.

When the Torah comes to a close, Moses climbs Mount Nebo and gazes out over the "land of milk and honey" that he will never set foot on. According to the literal biblical text, Moses dies silently and at peace. According to a midrashic legend, however, Moses resists, and his fighting spirit and combative nature appear to return to him. After being told that he is about to perish, Moses draws a circle around himself and informs God that he will not take another step unless God annuls the divine decree. He pleas, prays, begs not to die. The highest level of his soul, his neshamah, beseeches God not to be detached from the great prophet's body. Yet at long last, following soothing, loving words from his Creator, God gives Moses a kiss—one that draws his soul from this world to the next. He perseveres. In reaching his end, Moses has only found a new beginning.

Moses, Miriam, and most of the other key characters and events of the Exodus experience are recounted every year on the holiday of Passover, when we celebrate Israel's transition from slavery to freedom during the recitation of the Haggadah. For the mystics, *Mitzrayim* ("Egypt") was understood metaphorically, not as a particular region or regime, but as those narrow straits (*metzarim*) that hold us back from realizing our full potential, the inner enslavement that occurs when we let our egocentricity dominate us.

The Seder plate is one of the most important ritual objects of Passover, and *maror,* or bitter herbs, are one of its most essential features. By tradition, a person who has not consumed bitter herbs during the Passover Seder has not fulfilled his or her religious obligations. Yet why is maror considered so vital in the spiritual context? Rabbi Yaakov Yosef of Polonnoye, the Hasidic master we cited in the second chapter, explained that through eating bitter herbs we gain a better understanding of the role that "bitterness" can play in our internal development. Our base desires and self-centered natures are so strong that we can prevail over them only through the bitterness of the personal disappointments and seemingly endless struggles that we will all inevitably encounter throughout our lives. We are "toughened up" so as to transcend ourselves.

As provocative as this reasoning is, it rings very true to me. The bitter experience of adversity is, when viewed in this way, *necessary* for us to persevere and progress—not something to run away from, but an opportunity we should embrace with all our souls.

CONCLUSION

WHAT I HAVE tried to offer through this book is a path, not a panacea, a program of stages, not a magic potion. The road to becoming a spiritual warrior is a very difficult one, and it takes a lifetime of striving just to get close to its realization. I have been a rabbi for fifteen years, and I have practiced the martial arts for the same amount of time. During that period, I have learned from some of the great masters, from the words of long-dead sages to the lessons of contemporary teachers. And I know that I am still only a student on a quest, far from my objective, with miles and miles to go before I sleep.

We have explored, through the teachings and deeds of mystics, thinkers, biblical characters, philosophers, and modern people, the many and varied ways we can work toward self-empowerment and self-transcendence. I have shared several of my own experiences as well. In the end, it seems quite clear to me that there are some specific principles and practices that are shared by the most successful of spiritual seekers, and we have read nearly two hundred pages that illustrate how and why they seem to be so necessary:

- Openness
- Introspection
- Discipline
- Courage
- Creativity
- Stamina
- Restraint
- Perseverance

In the introduction, I asked what core qualities were essential in an authentic, fully attuned, and well-prepared spiritual warrior. My answers were the following: an understanding of, and mastery over, one's own soul; insight and perspective; and a sense of mission. The eight concepts and stages I've explained and the sequence in which they are aligned are the means by which we can—with effort—achieve these qualities.

Our very first step is to be receptive to and ready for anything, good or bad. When the inevitable occurs and we are faced with an adversary or an obstacle in life, our next task is assessment and identification: How powerful a threat is it that we are up against? What is the true nature of the enemy we must confront? Is it something external and around us, such as social injustice, oppression, abuse, or indifference? Or is it something *within* us, such as fear, anger, or our own narcissism and ego? A warrior must engage an opponent boldly and with self-confidence, trusting in his or her own ability and potential. The dimension and character of our adversaries will determine how we approach them.

Only with that insight can we properly use all we have learned, practiced, and experienced. Only then can we bring our humility, training, creativity, and will to an existential "war zone."

We must know which tactics to use in which situations. Our contexts—and contests—will vary and change, and we will constantly be tested in unexpected and unpredictable ways. Adaptability and endurance are our keys to success. Yet a victory for the spiritual warrior means more than simply vanquishing an opponent or surmounting a challenge. It means that the experience of struggle itself has led to inner growth, to the evolution and maturation of our own souls. And the morality of any mission must be beyond question; when we stand up for others, we simultaneously strengthen ourselves.

According to Ralph Waldo Emerson, "Our greatest glory is not in never falling, but in rising up every time we fall." This teaching is echoed by a Japanese proverb: "Fall seven times, stand up eight." Our nobility—the affirmation of the human spirit—resides in our soul's *indomitability*, its capacity to persevere. We will win some battles and lose others, but the spiritual warrior will fight on and understand that no victory is ever complete and the journey toward redemption is never over. Falling short of our goals is a natural, ongoing part of our progress. It is how we evolve as humans. Episodes of failure should serve as catalysts for acts of fortitude. Ends should unfold into fresh beginnings.

We live in a troubled era in which people are more confused and despondent than ever; several of the personal stories in this book illustrate just how deep into despair some of us can fall. But they also offer a message, anchored in ancient traditions, of direction, inspiration, and hope. As my own teachers have instructed me—and as they have given me experiences, skills, and weapons with which to confront the challenges of the human condition—this book and its program of self-empowerment is my opportunity to pass on those principles and practices (and that profound warrior wisdom) to a new generation.

None of these important and potentially life-altering teachings are inaccessible to any of us. Every human being possesses untapped and unrealized powers, abilities, and capacities to transform who we are, as well as to transcend where we are. The path of the spiritual warrior is as much an invitation as it is a challenge. It beckons for us to go further and deeper than most of us have ever gone before, to embark on an internal quest of self-discovery. It involves hard work, commitment, and sacrifice—and a willingness to open ourselves that will likely make many of us feel vulnerable. Yet that vulnerability will lead to vision. For, despite its daunting aspects, the warrior's path is one of great power and purpose, meant to guide us to more hopeful, fulfilling, and meaningful lives.

ACKNOWLEDGMENTS

There are several people I would like to thank for helping me with this book, but paramount among them is my editor, Beth Frankl. In an industry where personal attention and passionate commitment to literary projects have become so rare, Beth is a shining example of someone who counters the current trend. She is both attentive and impassioned, and I consider her a wonderful editor, advocate, and friend. I look forward to future projects together, and I can't think of too many other people who I'd rather have by my side. Thanks, Beth, and keep up the good fight.

I also want to express my deep appreciation to my visionary, tireless publisher, Peter Turner, and to Julie Saidenberg, Jennifer Campaniolo, Chloe Foster, and the rest of the amazing team at Trumpeter. I offer my gratitude for all of their hard work, great ideas, and support for this book. Not only are they consummate professionals; they are also good, spiritual people who actually "walk the walk." They *get* it.

As always, I am grateful to my agent, Linda Loewenthal, who continues to help me navigate the reefs and shoals of the book business. After another book together, I would like to thank you for your ongoing belief in and commitment to my work.

Finally, I would like to offer my heartfelt gratitude to all of my teachers from all the many and varied fields in which I have learned—but most of all to Michele, who has taught me more about being a spiritual warrior, about learning how to evolve, mature, and grow from life's challenges, than any of my other instructors and guides possibly could.

ABOUT THE AUTHOR

Niles Elliot Goldstein is the founder and Rabbi Emeritus of The New Shul, an innovative and independent congregation in Greenwich Village, New York. He lectures widely on religion and spirituality and has taught at New York University and the Hebrew Union College-Jewish Institute of Religion. Goldstein is the National Jewish Chaplain for the Federal Law Enforcement Officers Association, a member of PEN and the Renaissance Institute, and was the voice behind "Ask the Rabbi" on the Microsoft Network. His essays, op-ed pieces, and poetry have appeared in *Newsweek,* the *Los Angeles Times, Newsday,* and many other publications, and he is the award-winning author or editor of eight previous books. Goldstein has been featured in *Time,* the *New York Times,* the *Wall Street Journal,* the *Christian Science Monitor,* the *New York Observer, New York Magazine, Real Simple,* and *Glamour* as well as on national and international television and radio such as Dateline, CNN, MSNBC, NPR, Voice of America, and the BBC. He lives in Brooklyn, New York.